ROYAL COURT

Royal Court Theatre presents

WILD EAST

by **April De Angelis**

First performance at the Royal Court Jerwood Theatre Downstairs,
Sloane Square, London on 27 January 2005.

WILD EAST is supported by the ROYAL COURT'S PRODUCTION SYNDICATE.

WILD EAST

by **April De Angelis**

Cast
Frank **Tom Brooke**
Dr. Pitt **Sylvestra Le Touzel**
Dr. Gray **Helen Schlesinger**

Director **Phyllida Lloyd**
Designer **Mark Thompson**
Lighting Designer **Adam Silverman**
Sound Designer **Ian Dickinson**
Casting **Lisa Makin**
Production Manager **Paul Handley**
Stage Manager **Tariq Sayyid Rifaat**
Deputy Stage Manager **Rachel Barkataki**
Assistant Stage Manager **Hannah Dickinson**
Costume Supervisor **Iona Kenrick**
Company Voice Work **Patsy Rodenburg**
Set built by **Miraculous Engineering**

THE COMPANY

April De Angelis (writer)
For the Royal Court: Hush.
Theatre includes: A Laughing Matter (Out of Joint/
RNT/tour); The Warwickshire Testimony (RSC); The
Positive Hour (Out of Joint/Hampstead); Playhouse
Creatures (West Yorkshire Playhouse/Old Vic/
Sphinx); Headstrong (RNT Shell Connections).
Opera includes: Flight (Glyndebourne).

Tom Brooke
Theatre includes: Some Voices (Young Vic),
Four Little Plays Called Rape (Edinburgh/Etcetera).
Television includes: Coming Up, Rockabye, Murder
Prevention, D-Day Landings.
Film includes: The Libertine, Bridget Jones: The Edge
of Reason, The Happiness Thief.
Opera includes: Don Carlos, War and Peace.

Ian Dickinson (sound designer)
For the Royal Court: Shining City (& Gate, Dublin),
Lucky Dog, Blest Be the Tie (with Talawa TC),
Ladybird, Notes on Falling Leaves, Loyal Women,
The Sugar Syndrome, Blood, Playing the Victim
(with Told By an Idiot), Fallout, Flesh Wound,
Hitchcock Blonde (& Lyric), Black Milk,
Crazyblackmuthafuckin'self, Caryl Churchill Shorts,
Imprint, Mother Teresa is Dead, Push Up, Workers
Writes, Fucking Games, Herons, Cutting Through
the Carnival.
Other theatre includes: Port (Royal Exchange,
Manchester); Night of the Soul (RSC Barbican);
Eyes of the Kappa (Gate); Crime & Punishment in
Dalston (Arcola Theatre); Search & Destroy (New
End, Hampstead); Phaedra, Three Sisters,
The Shaughraun, Writer's Cramp (Royal Lyceum,
Edinburgh); The Whore's Dream (RSC Fringe,
Edinburgh); As You Like It, An Experienced Woman
Gives Advice, Present Laughter, The Philadelphia
Story, Wolk's World, Poor Superman, Martin
Yesterday, Fast Food, Coyote Ugly, Prizenight (Royal
Exchange, Manchester).
Ian is Head of Sound at the Royal Court.

Sylvestra Le Touzel
For the Royal Court: Glasshouses, Unity, Ourselves
Alone, My Heart's a Suitcase.
Other theatre includes: Strange Fruit (Sheffield
Crucible); Harvest (Ambassadors); The
Understanding (Strand); The War at Home, Fall,
Imagine Drowning (Hampstead); The London
Cuckolds, The Alchemist, Dracula (Lyric,
Hammersmith); The Wandering Jew, Countrymania
(RNT); The Fairy Queen (Aix Festival); Marya, The
Illusion (Old Vic); Hamlet, Henry IV Part 1, Twelfth
Night, A Woman Killed with Kindness, Artists and
Admirers, Les Enfants du Paradis (RSC);
An Inspector Calls (Aldwych); A Midsummer
Night's Dream (Almeida) Hay Fever (Savoy);
Benefactors (Albery/tour).
Television includes: Falling, Silent Witness, Judge
John Deed, Inspector Lowry, Lynley Mysteries,
A Family Affair, Hard Times, The Year Next Year,
Donal & Sally, Crimes, Mansfield Park, Naming the
Names, Between the Lines, The Gambling Man,
The Uninvited, Vanity Fair, Beast, Hearts & Bones,
Dual Balls.
Film includes: The Short and Curlies.
Radio includes: The Child that Books Built, The
Italian Detective, Killing Maestros, Nought Happens
Twice Thus, The Cloud Chamber, The Diaries of
Molly Panter Downes, Speaking for Themselves,
A Midsummer Night's Dream, The Merry Wives of
Windsor, Sea Urchins, The Airmen Who Wouldn't
Die, As You Like It.

Phyllida Lloyd (director)
For the Royal Court: Six Degrees of Separation,
Hysteria (& Duke of York's).
Other theatre includes: The Comedy of Errors,
A Streetcar Named Desire, Dona Rosita,
The Spinster, Oliver Twist (Bristol Old Vic); The
Winter's Tale, The School For Scandal, Death and
the King's Horseman, Medea (Royal Exchange,
Manchester); The Threepenny Opera, Boston
Marriage (Donmar Warehouse/West End); Dona
Rosita (Almeida); Pericles, What the Butler Saw, The
Way of the World, The Prime of Miss Jean Brodie,
The Duchess of Malfi (RNT); The Virtuoso, Artists
and Admirers (RSC); The Taming of the Shrew
(Globe); Mamma Mia! (Prince of Wales Theatre/
worldwide).
Opera includes: L'Etoile; La Boheme, Medea,
Carmen, Gloriana, Albert Herring (Opera North);
Macbeth (Opera National de Paris/Royal Opera
House/Liceu Barcelona); The Carmelites, Verdi
Requiem, Wagner's Ring (ENO); The Handmaid's
Tale (Royal Danish Opera, ENO, Canadian Opera).
Television includes: Gloriana, a film which won a
FIPA d'Or, the Royal Philharmonic Society Award
and an International Emmy.

Helen Schlesinger

For the Royal Court: The Weather, Bear Hug.
Other theatre includes: Messiah (Old Vic); Uncle
Vanya, A Moon for the Misbegotten, King Lear, The
Illusion, Road to Mecca (Royal Exchange); The
Oresteia, Inadmissible Evidence (RNT); The
Merchant of Venice, Twelfth Night (RSC); Mill on
the Floss, War and Peace (Shared Experience/
RNT); An Inspector Calls, Becket (RNT/West End);
No Experience Required (Hampstead); Foreign
Lands (Wolsey, Ipswich); The Europeans
(Greenwich and tour); The Winter's Tale,
The Second Mrs Tanqueray (Salisbury); Miss Julie
(Plymouth); Wild Oats (West Yorkshire Playhouse);
Design for Living, Don Juan (Harrogate); Hamlet,
Romeo and Juliet, Volpone, The Tempest (Compass
Theatre).
Television includes: Dirty War, Waking the Dead IV,
The Playground, Rose and Maloney, The Way We
Live Now, Bad Girls, The Greatest Store in the
World, Devil's Advocate, Between the Lines,
Harnessing Peacocks, Bad Girl.
Awards include: Best Actress in Manchester
Evening News Theatre Awards 2001 for A Moon
for the Misbegotten and Uncle Vanya.

Adam Silverman (lighting designer)
Theatre includes: The Shape of Things (New
Ambassadors); Five Gold Rings (Almeida); Beauty
and the Beast (RSC/Stratford); Giselle (Fabulous
Beast); Mayor of Zalamea (Liverpool Everyman);
A Day in the Life of Joe Egg (Broadway); This is
Our Youth (Garrick); The Three Musketeers,
'Tis Pity She's a Whore (Young Vic); The Three
Birds (Gate, London); Quartz (Traverse); The Cider
House Rules (Atlantic, NY); The New Bozena
(Cherry Lane, NY); Cyrano de Bergerac (Gate,
Dublin); Power Plays (Promenade, NY); Dark Ride
(SoHo Rep, NY).
Musicals include: One Touch of Venus (Opera
North); Moon Under Miami (Remains, Chicago).
Opera includes: Siegfried (ENO); Imeneo
(Glimmerglass Opera, NY); Eight Little Greats
(Opera North); Jenufa (Houston Grand Opera);
Der Schatzgräber (Oper Frankfurt); Pique Dame
(Bayerische Staatsoper, Munich); La Traviata (New
Israeli Opera, Tel Aviv).

Mark Thompson (designer)
For the Royal Court: Six Degrees of Separation (&
Comedy); Hysteria (& Mark Taper Forum, Los
Angeles); Never Land, The Kitchen, Mouth to
Mouth,
Other theatre includes: Insignificance, The Front
Page (Donmar); Uncle Vanya, Twelfth Night (costume
only, Donmar/BAM); Company (Donmar/Albery);
The Blue Room (Donmar/Broadway).Measure for
Measure, The Wizard of Oz, Much Ado About
Nothing, The Comedy of Errors, Hamlet, The
Unexpected Man (RSC); Volpone, Betrayal, Party
Time, Butterfly Kiss (Almeida); The Wind in the
Willows, The Madness of King George III, Pericles,
What the Butler Saw, The Day I Stood Still, The
Duchess of Malfi (RNT); Life x 3 (RNT/Old
Vic/Broadway); Arcadia (RNT/Haymarket/Lincoln
Center Theater, NY),Bombay Dreams (Apollo
Victoria/Broadway); Follies (Broadway); Mamma Mia!
(Prince of Wales/Prince Edward/Broadway/
international tours); The Lady in the Van (Queen's);
Dr Dolittle (London Apollo/tour); Blast (Apollo/US
tour/Broadway); Art (Wyndham's/UK tour, Australia,
Buenos Aires, Chicago, Los Angeles &
Broadway);Owners (Young Vic); Good (Brussels);
The Scarlet Pimpernel (Chichester/Her Majesty's);
The Sneeze (Aldwych); Ivanov, Cabaret, Much Ado
About Nothing (Strand); A Little Light Music
(Piccadilly); Shadowlands (Queen's/Broadway);
Joseph and the Amazing Technicolor Dreamcoat
(London Palladium/ Canadian, Australian & American
tours).
Opera includes: Falstaff (Scottish Opera); Peter
Grimes (Opera North); Ariadne Auf Naxos
(Salzburg); Il Viaggio A Reims (ROH); Hansel and
Gretel (Sydney Opera House); The Two Widows
(ENO); Queen of Spades (The Met, New York);
Montag aus Licht (costume only, La Scala Milan).
Ballet includes: Don Quixote (Royal Ballet).
Film includes: The Madness of King George
(costume design).
Awards include: 1990/91 Olivier Award; Plays and
Players and Critics' Award for The Wind in the
Willows; 1992 Olivier Awards for Set Design and
Costume Design for Joseph And The Amazing
Technicolor Dreamcoat and The Comedy Of Errors;
1994 Olivier Award for Set Design for Hysteria;
1995 Critics' Circle Award for The Kitchen; Olivier
Award nomination 2003 and Tony Award
nomination 2004 for Best Costume Designer for
Bombay Dreams.

THE ENGLISH STAGE COMPANY
AT THE ROYAL COURT

The English Stage Company at the Royal Court opened in 1956 as a subsidised theatre producing new British plays, international plays and some classical revivals.

The first artistic director George Devine aimed to create a writers' theatre, 'a place where the dramatist is acknowledged as the fundamental creative force in the theatre and where the play is more important than the actors, the director, the designer'. The urgent need was to find a contemporary style in which the play, the acting, direction and design are all combined. He believed that 'the battle will be a long one to continue to create the right conditions for writers to work in'.

Devine aimed to discover 'hard-hitting, uncompromising writers whose plays are stimulating, provocative and exciting'. The Royal Court production of John Osborne's Look Back in Anger in May 1956 is now seen as the decisive starting point of modern British drama and the policy created a new generation of British playwrights. The first wave included John Osborne, Arnold Wesker, John Arden, Ann Jellicoe, N F Simpson and Edward Bond. Early seasons included new international plays by Bertolt Brecht, Eugène Ionesco, Samuel Beckett, Jean-Paul Sartre and Marguerite Duras.

The theatre started with the 400-seat proscenium arch Theatre Downstairs, and in 1969 opened a second theatre, the 60-seat studio Theatre Upstairs. Some productions transfer to the West End, such as Terry Johnson's Hitchcock Blonde, Caryl Churchill's Far Away and Conor McPherson's The Weir. Recent touring productions include Sarah Kane's 4.48 Psychosis (US tour) and Ché Walker's Flesh Wound (Galway Arts Festival). The Royal Court also co-produces plays which have transferred to the West End or toured internationally, such as Conor McPherson's Shining City (with Gate Theatre, Dublin), Sebastian Barry's The Steward of Christendom and Mark Ravenhill's Shopping and Fucking (with Out of Joint), Martin McDonagh's The Beauty Queen Of Leenane (with Druid), Ayub Khan Din's East is East (with Tamasha).

Since 1994 the Royal Court's artistic policy has again been vigorously directed to finding and producing a new generation of playwrights. The writers include Joe Penhall, Rebecca Prichard, Michael Wynne, Nick Grosso, Judy Upton, Meredith Oakes, Sarah Kane, Anthony Neilson, Judith Johnson, James Stock, Jez Butterworth, Marina Carr, Phyllis Nagy, Simon Block, Martin McDonagh, Mark Ravenhill, Ayub Khan Din,

photo: Andy Chopping

Tamantha Hammerschlag, Jess Walters, Ché Walker, Conor McPherson, Simon Stephens, Richard Bean, Roy Williams, Gary Mitchell, Mick Mahoney, Rebecca Gilman, Christopher Shinn, Kia Corthron, David Gieselmann, Marius von Mayenburg, David Eldridge, Leo Butler, Zinnie Harris, Grae Cleugh, Roland Schimmelpfennig, Chloe Moss, DeObia Oparei, Enda Walsh, Vassily Sigarev, the Presnyakov Brothers, Marcos Barbosa, Lucy Prebble, John Donnelly, Clare Pollard, Robin French, Elyzabeth Gregory Wilder and Rob Evans. This expanded programme of new plays has been made possible through the support of A.S.K. Theater Projects and the Skirball Foundation, The Jerwood Charity, the American Friends of the Royal Court Theatre and (in 1994/5 and 1999) in association with the National Theatre Studio.

In recent years there have been record-breaking productions at the box office, with capacity houses for Joe Penhall's Dumb Show, Conor McPherson's Shining City, Roy Williams' Fallout and Terry Johnson's Hitchcock Blonde.

The refurbished theatre in Sloane Square opened in February 2000, with a policy still inspired by the first artistic director George Devine. The Royal Court is an international theatre for new plays and new playwrights, and the work shapes contemporary drama in Britain and overseas.

AWARDS FOR
ROYAL COURT

Jez Butterworth won the 1995 George Devine Award, the Writers' Guild New Writer of the Year Award, the Evening Standard Award for Most Promising Playwright and the Olivier Award for Best Comedy for Mojo.

The Royal Court was the overall winner of the 1995 Prudential Award for the Arts for creativity, excellence, innovation and accessibility. The Royal Court Theatre Upstairs won the 1995 Peter Brook Empty Space Award for innovation and excellence in theatre.

Michael Wynne won the 1996 Meyer-Whitworth Award for The Knocky. Martin McDonagh won the 1996 George Devine Award, the 1996 Writers' Guild Best Fringe Play Award, the 1996 Critics' Circle Award and the 1996 Evening Standard Award for Most Promising Playwright for The Beauty Queen of Leenane. Marina Carr won the 19th Susan Smith Blackburn Prize (1996/7) for Portia Coughlan. Conor McPherson won the 1997 George Devine Award, the 1997 Critics' Circle Award and the 1997 Evening Standard Award for Most Promising Playwright for The Weir. Ayub Khan Din won the 1997 Writers' Guild Awards for Best West End Play and New Writer of the Year and the 1996 John Whiting Award for East is East (co-production with Tamasha).

Martin McDonagh's The Beauty Queen of Leenane (co-production with Druid Theatre Company) won four 1998 Tony Awards including Garry Hynes for Best Director. Eugene Ionesco's The Chairs (co-production with Theatre de Complicite) was nominated for six Tony awards. David Hare won the 1998 Time Out Live Award for Outstanding Achievement and six awards in New York including the Drama League, Drama Desk and New York Critics Circle Award for Via Dolorosa. Sarah Kane won the 1998 Arts Foundation Fellowship in Playwriting. Rebecca Prichard won the 1998 Critics' Circle Award for Most Promising Playwright for Yard Gal (co-production with Clean Break).

Conor McPherson won the 1999 Olivier Award for Best New Play for The Weir. The Royal Court won the 1999 ITI Award for Excellence in International Theatre. Sarah Kane's Cleansed was judged Best Foreign Language Play in 1999 by Theater Heute in Germany. Gary Mitchell won the 1999 Pearson Best Play Award for Trust. Rebecca Gilman was joint winner of the 1999 George Devine Award and won the 1999 Evening Standard Award for Most Promising Playwright for The Glory of Living.

In 1999, the Royal Court won the European theatre prize New Theatrical Realities, presented at Taormina Arte in Sicily, for its efforts in recent years in discovering and producing the work of young British dramatists.

Roy Williams and Gary Mitchell were joint winners of the George Devine Award 2000 for Most Promising Playwright for Lift Off and The Force of Change respectively. At the Barclays Theatre Awards 2000 presented by the TMA, Richard Wilson won the Best Director Award for David Gieselmann's Mr Kolpert and Jeremy Herbert won the Best Designer Award for Sarah Kane's 4.48 Psychosis. Gary Mitchell won the Evening Standard's Charles Wintour Award 2000 for Most Promising Playwright for The Force of Change. Stephen Jeffreys' I Just Stopped by to See the Man won an AT&T: On Stage Award 2000.

David Eldridge's Under the Blue Sky won the Time Out Live Award 2001 for Best New Play in the West End. Leo Butler won the George Devine Award 2001 for Most Promising Playwright for Redundant. Roy Williams won the Evening Standard's Charles Wintour Award 2001 for Most Promising Playwright for Clubland. Grae Cleugh won the 2001 Olivier Award for Most Promising Playwright for Fucking Games. Richard Bean was joint winner of the George Devine Award 2002 for Most Promising Playwright for Under the Whaleback. Caryl Churchill won the 2002 Evening Standard Award for Best New Play for A Number. Vassily Sigarev won the 2002 Evening Standard Charles Wintour Award for Most Promising Playwright for Plasticine. Ian MacNeil won the 2002 Evening Standard Award for Best Design for A Number and Plasticine. Peter Gill won the 2002 Critics' Circle Award for Best New Play for The York Realist (English Touring Theatre). Ché Walker won the 2003 George Devine Award for Most Promising Playwright for Flesh Wound. Lucy Prebble won the 2003 Critics' Circle Award and the 2004 George Devine Award for Most Promising Playwright, and the TMA Theatre Award 2004 for Best New Play for The Sugar Syndrome. Linda Bassett won the 2004 TMA Theatre Award for Best Actress (for Leo Butler's Lucky Dog).

ROYAL COURT BOOKSHOP

The Royal Court bookshop offers a range of contemporary plays and publications on the theory and practice of modern drama. The staff specialise in assisting with the selection of audition monologues and scenes.
Royal Court playtexts from past and present productions cost £2.
The Bookshop is situated in the downstairs ROYAL COURT BAR AND FOOD.
Monday–Friday 3–10pm, Saturday 2.30–10pm
For information tel: 020 7565 5024
or email: bookshop@royalcourttheatre.com

PROGRAMME SUPPORTERS

The Royal Court (English Stage Company Ltd) receives its principal funding from Arts Council England, London. It is also supported financially by a wide range of private companies, charitable and public bodies, and earns the remainder of its income from the box office and its own trading activities.

The Genesis Foundation supports the International Season and Young Writers' Festival.

The Jerwood Charity supports new plays by new playwrights through the Jerwood New Playwrights series. The Skirball Foundation funds a Playwrights' Programme at the theatre. The Artistic Director's Chair is supported by a lead grant from The Peter Jay Sharp Foundation, contributing to the activities of the Artistic Director's office. Bloomberg Mondays, the Royal Court's reduced price ticket scheme, is supported by Bloomberg. Over the past eight years the BBC has supported the Gerald Chapman Fund for directors.

ROYAL COURT
DEVELOPMENT BOARD
Tamara Ingram
(Chair)
Jonathan Cameron
(Vice Chair)
Timothy Burrill
Anthony Burton
Jonathan Caplan QC
Sindy Caplan
Mark Crowdy
Cas Donald
Joseph Fiennes
Joyce Hytner OBE
Gavin Neath
Michael Potter
Ben Rauch
Kadee Robbins
Mark Robinson
William Russell
Sue Stapely
James L Tanner
Will Turner

PUBLIC FUNDING
Arts Council England,
London
British Council
Creative Partnerships
London South
London Challenge
Royal Borough of
Kensington & Chelsea

TRUSTS AND
FOUNDATIONS
American Friends of the
Royal Court Theatre
Gerald Chapman Fund
Cowley Charitable
Trust
The Dorset
Foundation
The Ronald Duncan
Literary Foundation
The Foundation for
Sport and the Arts
The Foyle Foundation
Francis Finlay
Foundation
The Garfield Weston
Foundation
Genesis Foundation

The Haberdashers'
Company
Jerwood Charity
John Lyon's Charity
The Magowan Family
Foundation
The Moose Foundation
for the Arts
The Laura Pels
Foundation
Quercus Charitable
Trust
The Rayne Foundation
The Royal Victoria Hall
Foundation.
The Peter Jay Sharp
Foundation
Skirball Foundation
The Bruce Wake
Charitable Trust

SPONSORS
Giorgio Armani
Arts & Business New
Partners
Barclays
BBC
Bloomberg
City Inn, Westminster
Peter Jones

BUSINESS AND MEDIA
MEMBERS
Aviva plc
Bloomsbury
Columbia Tristar Films
(UK)
Hat Trick Productions
Lazard
Pemberton Greenish
Simons Muirhead &
Burton
Slaughter and May

PRODUCTION
SYNDICATE
Anonymous
The Albano Family
Jonathan & Sindy
Caplan
Mrs Philip Donald
Peter & Edna
Goldstein

Jack & Linda Keenan
Richard & Robin
Landsberger
Kadee Robbins
The Viscount &
Viscountess
Rothermere
William & Hilary
Russell
Kay Hartenstein Saatchi
Jon and NoraLee
Sedmak
James & Victoria
Tanner
Jan & Michael Topham

INDIVIDUAL MEMBERS
Patrons
Anonymous
Dr Bettina Bahisen
Katie Bradford
Marcus J Burton
Ms Kay Ellen
Consolver
Celeste Fenichel
Tom & Simone Fenton
Jack & Linda Keenan
Duncan Matthews QC
Ian & Carol Sellars
Jan & Michael Topham
Richard Wilson OBE

Benefactors
Anonymous
Martha Allfrey
Varian Ayers & Gary
Knisely
John & Anoushka
Ayton
Lucy Bryn Davies
Jeremy Conway &
Nicola Van Gelder
Robyn Durie
Joachim Fleury
Tamara Ingram
Peter & Maria Kellner
Barbara Minto
Brian D Smith
Sue Stapeley
Amanda Vail
Sir Robert &
Lady Wilson
Nick Wheeler

Associates
Act IV
Anonymous
Jeffrey Archer
Brian Boylan
Alan Brodie
Ossi & Paul Burger
Mrs Helena Butler
Lady Cazalet
Carole & Neville
Conrad
David & Susan
Coppard
Margaret Cowper
Andrew Cryer
Linda & Ronald F. Daitz
David Day
Zoë Dominic
Kim Dunn
Charlotte & Nick Fraser
Gillian Frumkin
Jacqueline &
Jonathan Gestetner
Vivien Goodwin
Judy & Frank Grace
Don & Sue Guiney
P. Hobbs - LTRC
David & Suzie Hyman
Mrs Ellen Josefowitz
David Kaskel &
Christopher Teano
Mr & Mrs Tarek
Kassem
Carole A. Leng
Lady Lever
Colette & Peter Levy
Mr Watcyn Lewis
David Marks
Nicola McFarland
Gavin & Ann Neath
Georgia Oetker
Mr & Mrs Michael Orr
Pauline Pinder
William Poeton CBE &
Barbara Poeton
Jan & Michael Potter
Jeremy Priestley
Beverley Rider
John Ritchie
Lois Sieff OBE
Gail Steele
Will Turner
Anthony Wigram

THE AMERICAN FRIENDS OF THE ROYAL COURT THEATRE

AFRCT supports the mission of the Royal Court and are primarily focused on raising funds to enable the theatre to produce new work by emerging American writers. Since this not-for-profit organisation was founded in 1997, AFRCT has contributed to ten productions. It has also supported the participation of young artists in the Royal Court's acclaimed International Residency.

If you would like to support the ongoing work of the Royal Court, please contact the Development Department on 020 7565 5050.

Founders
Francis Finlay
Amanda Foreman &
Jonathan Barton
Monica Gerard-Sharp &
Ali Wambold
Blythe Masters
Laura Pels
Ben Rauch & Margaret
Scott
Mr & Mrs Gerald
Schoenfeld

Patrons
Catherine Curran
William & Ursula
Fairbairn
Francis H Goldwyn
Mr & Mrs Richard Grand
Sahra Lese
Imelda Liddiard

Benefactors
Rachael Bail
David Day & John
Drummond
Jeff & Cynthia Penney
Timothy Runion &
Vipul Nishawala
Mika Sterling
Mr & Mrs Robert G
Donnalley

Members
Harry Brown & Richard
Walsh
Georgiana Ellis
Nancy Flinn
Jennifer R Gardner
Sharon King Hope
Nancy Lamb
Rochelle Ohrstom
Evelyn Renold
Roberta Schneidermann
Patricia Shea
David & Patricia Smalley

Corporations & Foundations
American Express
Company
The Blessing Way
Foundation
The Edmond de
Rothschild Foundation
The Howard Gilman
Foundation
The Lone Pine
Foundation
The Magowan Family
Foundation
The Patchwork
Charitable Foundation
Proskauer Rose LLP
The Laura Pels
Foundation
The Shubert
Organization
The Sy Syms
Foundation
Union Pacific
Corporation

American Friends
Development Director
Timothy Runion
Tel: 001 212 946 5724

ROYAL COURT
SLOANE SQUARE

Jerwood Theatre Downstairs

1–23 April 7.30pm
STONING MARY

by
debbie tucker green
Directed by
Marianne Elliott

Supported by
JERWOOD NEW PLAYWRIGHTS

Jerwood Theatre Upstairs

24 February–19 March 7.45pm
BREATHING CORPSES

by **Laura Wade**
Directed by
Anna Mackmin

Supported by
JERWOOD NEW PLAYWRIGHTS

BOX OFFICE
020 7565 5000
BOOK ONLINE
www.royalcourttheatre.com

ARTS COUNCIL
ENGLAND

FOR THE ROYAL COURT

Royal Court Theatre, Sloane Square, London SW1W 8AS
Tel: 020 7565 5050 Fax: 020 7565 5001
info@royalcourttheatre.com
www.royalcourttheatre.com

Artistic Director **Ian Rickson**
Associate Director International **Elyse Dodgson**
Associate Director **Marianne Elliott**+
Associate Director Casting **Lisa Makin**
Associate Directors* **Stephen Daldry, Ramin Gray, James Macdonald, Katie Mitchell, Max Stafford-Clark, Richard Wilson**
Literary Manager **Graham Whybrow**
Pearson Playwright **Lucy Prebble**†
Literary Associate **Terry Johnson***
Voice Associate **Patsy Rodenburg***
Casting Deputy **Amy Ball**
International Associate **Tiffany Watt-Smith**
International Administrator **Chris James**
Artistic Assistant **Polly Wines**

Production Manager **Paul Handley**
Deputy Production Manager **Sue Bird**
Production Assistant **Sarah Davies**
Facilities Manager **Fran McElroy**
Head of Lighting **Johanna Town**
Lighting Deputy **Trevor Wallace**
Lighting Assistants **Gavin Owen, Nicki Brown**
Lighting Board Operator **Kelli Marston**
Head of Stage **Martin Riley**
Stage Deputy **Steven Stickler**
Stage Chargehand **Daniel Lockett**
Head of Sound **Ian Dickinson**
Sound Deputy **Emma Laxton**
Head of Costume **Iona Kenrick**
Deputy Head of Costume **Jackie Orton**

YOUNG WRITERS PROGRAMME
Associate Director **Ola Animashawun**
Administrator **Nina Lyndon**
Outreach Worker **Lucy Dunkerley**
Education Officer **Emily McLaughlin**
Writers Tutor **Simon Stephens***

General Manager **Diane Borger**
Administrator **Ushi Bagga**
Finance Director **Sarah Preece**
Finance Officer **Rachel Harrison***
Finance Officer **Martin Wheeler**
Finance Manager **Steve Eames***

Head of Marketing **Penny Mills**
Head of Press **Ewan Thomson**
Marketing Officer **Alix Hearn**
Press Officer **Lyndsay Roberts**
Box Office Manager **Neil Grutchfield**
Deputy Box Office Manager **Valli Dakshinamurthi**
Assistant Box Office Manager **Glen Bowman**
Box Office Sales Operators **Louise Kelly, Steven Kuleshnyk, Hannah McCarthy,**

Head of Development **Helen Salmon**
Trusts and Foundations Manager **Nicky Jones**
Development Manager **Leona Felton**
Development Officer **Natalie Moss**
Development Intern **Pam Wilson**

Theatre Manager **Elizabeth Brown**
Deputy Theatre Manager **Bobbie Stokes**
Front of House Manager **Nathalie Meghriche**
Duty House Managers* **Matt Tallen, David Duchin**
Bookshop Manager **Simon David**
Assistant Bookshop Manager **Edin Suljic***
Bookshop Assistant* **Nicki Welburn**
Stage Door/Reception **Simon David, Jon Hunter, Tyrone Lucas, Paul Lovegrove**

Thanks to all of our box office assistants and ushers.

+ The Associate Director post is supported by the BBC through the Gerald Chapman Fund.
† This theatre has the support of the Pearson Playwright's Scheme sponsored by Pearson plc.
* Part-time.

ENGLISH STAGE COMPANY

President
Sir John Mortimer CBE QC

Vice President
Dame Joan Plowright CBE

Honorary Council
Sir Richard Eyre CBE
Alan Grieve CBE

Council
Chairwoman **Liz Calder**
Vice Chairman **Anthony Burton**

Members
Judy Daish
Graham Devlin
Joyce Hytner OBE
Tamara Ingram
Stephen Jeffreys
Phyllida Lloyd
James Midgley
Edward Miliband
Sophie Okonedo
Katharine Viner

April De Angelis
Wild East

faber and faber

First published in 2005
by Faber and Faber Limited
3 Queen Square London WC1N 3AU

Typeset by Country Setting, Kingsdown, Kent CT14 8ES
Printed in England by Mackays of Chatham plc, Chatham, Kent

All rights reserved
© April De Angelis, 2005

The right of April De Angelis to be identified as author
of this work has been asserted in accordance with Section 77
of the Copyright, Designs and Patents Act 1988

All rights whatsoever in this work, amateur or professional,
are strictly reserved. Applications for permission for any use
whatsoever, including performance rights, must be made in advance,
prior to any such proposed use, to Casarotto Ramsay and Associates Ltd,
National House, 60-66 Wardour Street, London W1V 4ND.
No performance may be given unless a licence has first been obtained.

This book is sold subject to the condition that it shall not,
by way of trade or otherwise, be lent, resold, hired out
or otherwise circulated without the publisher's prior consent
in any form of binding or cover other than that in which
it is published and without a similar condition including
this condition being imposed on the subsequent purchaser

A CIP record for this book
is available from the British Library

ISBN 0-571-22816-X

2 4 6 8 10 9 7 5 3 1

Characters

Frank

Dr Pitt

Dr Gray

WILD EAST

An anonymous, corporate room. Some papers on a round, low table surrounded by three chairs. The table has a coffee pot and three cups and also a sculptured centrepiece. There is a camera in the room operated by an on/off switch which is hand-held. Dr Pitt, who has her arm bandaged, stands regarding the room. She has not been on the premises for six weeks. It has cost her something to come back. Frank, a young man, enters. He has been hurrying. He sees Dr Pitt.

Frank This is Room 212?

Pitt Yes, it is.

Frank I thought I was going to be late. There was a defective train at Mile End or someone had been pushed onto the tracks. I couldn't quite make it out.

Pitt Maybe it was both.

Frank You're here for an interview?

Pitt Yes, I am.

Frank It's a strange time. 6 p.m. Why do you think they did that?
  Is it a disorientation technique?

Pitt I expect so.

Frank Possibly it's a body-clock thing, to push you. Normally, physically, you're clocking off about now.

Pitt I expect you're right.

Frank They're bastards. That's what my professor told me.

Beat.

Hello. I'm Frank.

Pitt Hello. I'm Dr Pitt. I shall be interviewing you in approximately two minutes.

Frank Oh, Jesus.

Pitt It's OK.

Frank Oh, shit.

Pitt Really. It is.

Frank Shit.

Pitt Frank. The interview hasn't started.

Frank Really?

Pitt Yes. You know what? I understand. I'm a human being too.
   We all make mistakes. In fact I'm flattered, Frank, that you should consider me young enough to be a candidate.

Frank They do take old people. Nowadays it's practically legislated for.

Pitt Can I give you some advice? The first thing that pops into your head may not always be appropriate.

Frank Right.

Pitt You don't always have to say what you feel, you know?

Frank OK.

Pitt Take the tip and you'll get through with flying colours.

Frank Thank you.

   Beat.

Pitt So, tell me. What exactly is this interview for?

Frank You mean you don't know?

Pitt I've been away. I slot back into things very fast.

Frank That's kind of unnerving. I mean from my perspective.

Pitt Don't worry about it, Frank. Fill me in.

Frank Well, your corporation is taking on the brightest of this year's graduates. We're fresh blood. We're hungry. We have all the new ideas.

Pitt What are they?

Frank Well, they're, you know, new.

Pitt Yeah, well, good luck. We could do with them. Are you hungry, Frank?

Frank I just ate.

Pitt For the work.

Frank Oh, yes.

Pitt But you wouldn't undercut someone's job at a reduced salary intake?

Frank No. What do you . . .? I mean. What? No.

Pitt Because if I suspect so, Frank, I will not be trying to get you through this.

Frank Oh. OK. Shit.

Dr Gray enters. She stops short at seeing Dr Pitt.

Gray God, you're here.
    And you must be Frank. I'm Dr Gray. I see you've met my colleague, Dr Pitt. We weren't sure that Dr Pitt would make it today. We're very glad to she did. Please sit down.

They sit.

Welcome.

Frank Hello.

Gray You speak Japanese.

Frank I did a crash course.

Gray And Russian. Congratulations, that's unusual.

Frank Thank you.

Gray How do you feel about Russia?

Frank Over the years I've come to love and admire the Russian people, their soul.

Gray About working there, I meant.

Frank I'd like to work there. I'd be very interested in a placement there.

Pause.

Would you like me to say more?

Pitt There's more?

Gray If you like.

Frank I keep an eye on Russia, so to speak.

Pitt I'm sure the Russians find that reassuring.

Frank I have friends I'm in regular contact with on the net.

Gray Informal networks can be valuable.

Frank And also fun.

Beat.

Do you want me to speak about the socio-economic developments, especially since the crisis of '98? I can do that.

Gray That's OK, Frank. We know you have a lot riding on this.

Our field is the most innovative and exciting development in the business world. Our client base has increased exponentially at a rate we could never have anticipated five years ago. What delights us is the opportunity to work with graduates from, in your case – (*She checks her notes.*) – the University of Lampeter. Well done for getting this far, Frank. This interview is your last hurdle.

Frank I'm practically birthing a kitten.

Gray This is a new carpet.

They laugh.

Pitt Can I ask a question?

Frank Sure.

Pitt Soul.

Frank What?

Pitt Where do you get off using the word 'soul', Frank? What is that? An attempt to impress us? You don't want to know what I wrote on my little piece of paper when you said that.

Frank It's a word the Russians use about themselves: *dusha.*

Pitt The Russians? What is that in the context of diverse populations except soft racism? I need coffee. (*She pours a cup with difficulty.*)

Frank My girlfriend is Russian.

Gray What I think Dr Pitt is pointing out is a central tenet in our research strategy, which is local focus. Time and again our studies in the field have turned up surprises for our clients. Let me give you an example. In the early days our company was approached by an outdoor clothing manufacturer. Our anthropologists identified thirty-six women who had an enthusiastic interest in the outdoors and conducted interviews with them about their lives and activities in the countryside. They made an unexpected discovery.

Beat.

Frank Were they involved in some kind of pagan ritual with sacrificial overtones?

Pitt This is Surrey, Frank. Don't get yours hopes up.

Gray Almost every respondent talked of going to a farmers' market. A marketing venue our client had never considered. Not a huge finding, but if you're an outdoor wear manufacturer . . . you couldn't go wrong with a booth at a farmers' market. They would never have figured that out.

Frank Yes, I see.

Pitt This coffee is shit. What made you turn to anthropology as a young person, Frank?

Frank Well, this may sound a little odd, but I confused it with archaeology and while related to archaeology it wasn't archaeology.

Pitt Help us out, Frank. There are X amount of candidates here today.
We'd like to think we had a winner.

Frank I'm just a little nervous.

Gray Can we talk about the camera?

Frank The camera?

Gray The interview is being recorded to facilitate selection. All candidates were informed of this procedure by letter.

Frank Oh, yes.

Gray The camera is operated manually in this room. Are there any questions?

Frank Does that mean we can switch it off?

Pitt Under presentation skills your application reads 'Excellent'.

Frank I didn't know what else to put.

Pitt I can think of several things.

Gray Good. We'll start. I'm switching on the camera. Frank, what do you know about yoghurt?

Frank Yoghurt? I'm allergic.

Pitt Ethnologically.

Frank Oh, God.

Gray Yoghurt was discovered two thousand years ago, by a mogul warrior who allowed milk to transform in a pouch during a desert journey. The name 'yoghurt' is Turkish and means 'life'. You say 'yoghurt' anywhere in the world and they'll know what you're talking about.

Frank I'll have to try it.

Gray It's a player; the fastest-growing product in the Russian dairy market, worth a billion dollars per annum.

Frank Wow.

Gray How might you begin to hypothesise a notional strategy of product placement in the present Russian climate?

Frank I don't really eat yoghurt. I get these red, itchy lumps. Hives.

Pitt You're going have to think, Frank, about what you know about the Russian *dusha* at the present time and apply that to yoghurt.

Frank Well, I'd say, I'd say . . . that . . . there's a feeling of loss, yes.

A feeling that something has been lost and a sense of things being out of control.

Pitt How can you be sure, Frank, that that's not just what you're projecting?

Maybe Russians are perfectly happy. There's X million of them.

Frank The Russian male has the earliest death rate in the developed world, forty-nine years, I believe. That's a lot to do with a sense of lost identity and also vodka.

Gray The unhappy Russian man, I buy that. Let's allow that your hypothesis is supported empirically. What kind of yoghurt might you expect these people to buy?

Frank Alcoholic yoghurt?

Pitt Russian yoghurt, Frank. Russian. In such circumstances it would be a fair conjecture that foreign yoghurt will not appeal as much as traditional brands.

Gray Our clients are foreign producers. They wanted to break into the Russian market. In a Russia reeling from a kind of a trauma, we found that to succeed the product would need the additional brand values of trustworthiness, paternalism, old Russia regenerated.

Frank All in one tub?

Gray We made these suggestions to our clients. They transformed them into images, slogans. Any guesses as to what they came up with?

Frank Um . . .

Beat.

Gray It was a bear.

Frank Yeah?

Gray A happy Russian bear in a forest eating a yoghurt. Now, it's outstripping home brands.

Pitt Any illuminating comments?

Frank Not really.

Pitt We're going have to push you here, Frank. This is an interview.

Frank I suppose a Russian might buy a yoghurt with a bear on because they think it will somehow improve their life. Except it's hard to think of a scenario where a dairy product could do that.

Gray There is an argument for targeting, Frank, it says a corporation might as well produce a product people are going to find attractive to buy.

Pitt Maybe you don't approve of the work of the company?

Gray He isn't saying that.

Pitt Maybe you could let the candidate answer the question. What are you saying, Frank?

Frank I'm just saying I have friends and that bear is lying.

Pitt The bear is fictional, it's a cartoon. It lacks a controlling mind.

Frank It's not really going to cheer them up.

Pitt Nothing is going to cheer them up. They're Russian, for Christ sakes!

Frank Sorry. Could I take a minute or two before we continue? I realise I've been opening my mouth and not knowing what's going to come out.

Gray We can certainly give you a minute or two.

Frank Thank you.

> *He exits.*
> *Dr Gray switches off the camera.*

Pitt Fuck my aunt.

Gray Give him a chance.

Pitt He only lacks a facial tic.

Gray You haven't read his scores?

Pitt Who've Marcia and Marco got? A high-flyer?

Gray You should read them.

Pitt I'm back. My six weeks are up. I'm in here with a hopeless loser. Failure is contagious. It rubs off. Maybe they never wanted me back?

Gray Don't be paranoid.

Pitt I bumped into Marcia just now. She looked at me like I had the word 'fucked' scribbled on my forehead. I refuse to be rationalised. I want my job. I deserve it. I'm good at it.

Gray That is paranoid.

Pitt Would they put anybody with me that they weren't thinking of rationalising too? Or are you in on it?

Gray It's good to see you, too. If what you say has any truth in it, don't give them an excuse by falling apart. And read his scores. (*She hands over paper.*) Maybe if you did a little homework you might have a clearer idea of the big picture. (*Reads.*) He's the best candidate. I chose him. Let's hope you haven't scared him off.

Frank re-enters.

Frank I'm ready to continue.

Gray Excellent, Frank. (*She switches on camera.*) In this next part of the interview the questions are more probing. You will be asked for personal details. Are you OK with that?

Frank Fine. I'm fine with that.

Gray We're interested in your actual lived experience because from past behaviour we can ascertain future behaviour. Can you tell us about a situation where you were presented with a problem you had no idea how to solve and how you eventually solved it? Just take all the time you need.

Frank OK.

Pitt Maybe you never solved anything?

Frank No, I did. My first visit to Siberia I got off the train. I wanted to experience something. I met some guys and I went back with them to their flat and we started to drink. Can I emphasise that drink isn't a particular thing with me, it's what students do.

Pitt We were students once, Frank.

Frank It was a tiny flat with one room and while we were drinking their mother was sleeping in a bed in the corner of the same room.
This was a tiny town on the edge of nothing much and these guys said there was nothing to do there except drink and buy pirate CDs. And we listened to Lou Reed and we drank and after a while I said I had to go and they said go where and I said I just have to go because I had

started to think who are these guys, and a while back one of them had taken out a knife to cut up a piece of bread. So I left and I was standing in the middle of this place and it was summer, so it wasn't cold but it was dark, and I thought I would go and walk in the forest to clear my head and then I would go to the station and wait for a train. I walked to the edge of this forest and I sat and watched the sun come up, the most enormous sun, and then I felt I would just take a look in the forest. And then you know what happened next? One bit of forest looks exactly like another and, Jesus, I started to realise those guys in the flat had had my interests at heart when they tried to stop me because, well, no one knew I was in the forest and it probably covered a thousand miles and I was lost in it and after eight hours I began to cry and I thought I am never going to get out of here alive. I thought how stupid I was And how I would miss people and how thirsty I was. Then I must have fallen asleep because I woke up and it was much colder and darker and one of my eyes must have been bitten 'cos I couldn't open it, and I became convinced I was going to die for real, and then I thought I better make the most of my last hours so I sucked some dew off some leaves and I just lay looking up at the trees and I realised that at least I was dying in the most beautiful place on the earth. Because this forest was, well, very beautiful and this time as the sun came up I could hear birds. And then I realised that I was being a prick and I had to make an effort so I dragged myself up and I chose a direction. I just made a choice and I walked and walked and two hours later I was at the train station.

Pitt And what learning did you take away from that experience?

Frank This is going to sound a little – but life is precious and beautiful.
   Also, always carry a mobile phone.

Gray Tell us about a situation where you attempted to improve something and you had to live with the consequences.

Pause.

Pitt Or maybe you never tried to improve on anything?

Frank No, I did. Alcohol is a common drug of choice amongst the student population. It was the choice of my friend, Brian. Brian was the shape of a mountain and maybe that was why he was slightly ostracised in our group. He always insisted on T-shirts even in winter, which I thought was a mistake taking into account his figure. And mainly the same T-shirt brown with a red 'Five' on the back and 'Triple Five Soul' in red lettering on the front. Sometimes this would alternate with another T-shirt which said 'Avez-vous a cuppa?' I often wanted to say to him you got to do something about your T-shirts, man – but I never had the guts. Mainly because no one else talked to us much, we hung out a lot together. And in the evenings we drank like bastards and we would talk about other people in the group and how they bored us or Brian would tell me all about his life. How disappointed he was when he found out he was not related to his own pet. How his mother fostered disturbed teenagers and one girl called Tina provided Brian with his first sexual experience and then wrote about it in a radio play which won a competition for young people and was broadcast on Radio Four.

My coursework began to suffer and my parents pulled me up on it and said we are not paying for you to get off your head every night. That night Brian called for me and I had to explain that I wasn't going anywhere till my work improved and even I could see the wisdom of that. So he went away. And he came back the next night and he went away and so on. Then Brian disappeared from tutorials so I went to see him. When he opened the door he said what the fuck do you want? And I said I'm worried about you, man, and he said do you want a cup of tea? So I went in and had one and I noticed his room was more chaotic than normal. And when he gave me my cup of tea there was a baked bean in it. His T-shirt was practically crackling with dirt. Brian, I said, what is it, man? And he said I don't know I guess I'm depressed and I said go to speak to someone. What about, he said. Whatever, I said. And then there was a silence and I said I was sorry about not drinking and he said he understood about the grades and everything, and then he said he had been doing something and I said what and he said he'd been injecting stuff into one of his feet. I said what kind of stuff and he said any stuff he could find. I said Jesus and he said do you want to take a look and I couldn't think of anything else to say so I said OK and it was – (*Beat.*) Well, a horrible sight. Like a streaky beaten-up melon or something and I said doesn't it hurt and he said yes it's fucking agony. I don't know what made this story come into my head.

Pitt Neither do I, Frank.

Gray What happened?

Frank His mother came and took him away.

Gray Did you do the right thing?

Frank Did I?

Gray What do you think?

Frank I don't know. Brian disappeared. I wrote to his mother and she wrote back.

One morning she went up to his room and a bag had gone and so had both of his T-shirts. Now she's always going to train stations and hanging about just in case she can get a sight of him. It was like he was getting more and more lost till he finally disappeared altogether.

Gray Thank you, Frank. That was a very honest reply. (*She switches off camera.*)

Pitt I'm going to be honest with you, Frank.
Do you know the images you have left me with? That you have placed in my head? Do you think when they are discussing candidates they will say, 'I know, let's take the guy who spoke about the diseased and puffy foot'? Remember they may be having lunch. Are these examples appropriate?

Frank I'm asking myself the same question, Dr Pitt. It could either be that I'm nervous or stupid.

Pitt You know this organisation is not looking for stupid nervous people.
It's not as if you've been instructed to give inappropriate replies?

Frank No.

Pitt In order to sabotage?

Frank No.

Gray These questions . . .

Pitt Because I am wondering what I am doing on my first day back and I am presented with you. I am even beginning to think this is all a sinister plot to make me look bad.

Frank That's ridiculous.

Pitt What?

Frank I'm not making you look bad on purpose. It's accidental.

Pitt You may look good on paper, Frank, but in life you're the blind date where I climb out the toilet window.

Gray Don't approach the candidate in a threatening manner.

Frank Dr Pitt is right. I do need to work on my interpersonal skills.

Pitt That is one aspect of a much wider problem, yes.

Frank I just thought of an answer to an earlier question. May I?

Pitt It won't help.

Frank After my initial mistake I just thought I'd go along with the idea of anthropology. I was in a weird kind of place in my head. I didn't really know what I wanted. I used to get up in the morning, dress, eat, go to college, listen to my professors, and I would think this is kind of interesting. I'm OK. I'm young. It's unlikely that I should be struck by a terminal illness. I have food, people around me. I listen to music, I liked my life, it was easy, I was in a pleasant kind of dream. But then that was what my parents had always told me.

You're in a kind of dream. What are you doing with your life? But I always said, I'm OK, I'm OK. I know my name.

And then I had to go to a site. The Omsk site.

We were lucky to get the chance, our professors said.

I remember on the plane over I fell asleep the whole way and the others were laughing at me and saying how could you fall asleep the whole way? And I don't remember anything much after that, except it was cold. And then of course it happened.

It was my turn to be at the site and taking notes for the group.

There was a man digging in a small pit and I was sitting on a crate and I was watching him. He was wearing a puffy jacket.

Suddenly he made a kind of noise in his throat and I wasn't sure if he had called me or not so I stood up. I watched him and he was paying great attention to a small patch of earth and he was scratching at it with his fingers and brushing at it with a small brush. After a long bit he stood up and he was holding something in the palm of his hand and he made another noise in his throat so I went down to him to see what was going on. When I looked at him there were tears rolling down his cheeks and he held this yellow lump of rock out to me.

And he said absolutely nothing because he was crying.

What is it? I said.

And then he looked at me like I was another species and he said it's a bird, can't you see? It's a bird.

And I looked and I couldn't see it. It was just a lump of yellow.

And that was the moment when I began to feel bad.

And at that moment it was as if word had spread and everyone knew because suddenly people appeared around us and they were all talking about the bird and that was the talk for the whole night and for weeks and still that talk is going on somewhere now.

But I began to think, well, why couldn't I see the bird.

And I began to think that I was less than other people like not human or something and I went off my food and my sleep and I forgot to wash and I suppose I became depressed and I cursed my luck that I was the one that had to be there when the bastard bird was found because now I felt deficient.

People about me started to notice because quite frankly I stank and I wandered round the camp at night. Then one night I bumped into the guy that had dug the bird up and he said to me did I want to take a look and I said yes and in my mind I was thinking well maybe I could do something to the bird like break it or steal it – something crazy like that, so he took me to the big tent and there it was, on a little piece of cloth with a little tag lying next to it. First I saw the feathers because there were feathers scored into the stone as if the wings were swept back against its body and then I followed the slender neck up to the head with the curved beak which was reaching forward because the bird was definitely diving, suggesting it was a water bird. It was carved by hand from mammoth ivory and smooth from constant handling, it was thirty thousand years old and I realised I was looking at the most beautiful thing I had ever seen. And it pierced me to the heart.

Who were the people that made it? Then I knew why I was doing my subject.

Beat.

It's been good to meet you both. (*He makes to leave.*)

Pitt Wait a minute. That was a moving explanation, Frank.

Frank Thank you.

Pitt Anthropology, the study of man. So what are you doing here, Frank? In anthropologist's hell?

Frank I think I explained in my application, Dr Pitt.

Pitt I have failed to read the applications, Frank.

Frank I have a strong personal tie to Russia and I was hoping to be able to work there. My girlfriend is head of the Institute of Anthropology in Novosibirsk. I was hoping to be able to complement my work for the company with work on a site of special anthropological interest in Siberia.

Gray That's not what you wrote on your application.

Frank No. This is the real reason.

Pitt Perhaps we should be congratulating you on your honesty, Frank. You showed us the face, not the mask. The etymology is revealing. 'Persona' is the Greek word for mask. It's an interesting thought as to whether human society has ever been able to exist without them. What do you think, Amelia?

Gray I think you like to think we're all wearing masks, but with most people what you see is what you get.

Pitt That's what you can expect from a Doctor of Business and Marketing Strategies.

Do you really want this, Frank? I'm giving you a chance here to get the hell out.

Gray Do you want me to log this?

Pitt You're a nerd. You should be tucked away in a dusty institution researching the sexual practices of early hunter-gathers.

Frank I felt I had no choice, Dr Pitt. I'm kind of *persona non grata* at my university, and that kind of thing means it's hard to get research posts.

And there aren't many of those in our field, let's face it.

Pitt What did you do, Frank?

Frank I didn't do anything. I came under suspicion. This isn't in my application.

Gray No.

Frank One day they walked into the tent and the bird had gone. Nothing. Just a dent in its cloth. Everyone was searched. Nothing was found. There were rumours of art theft. Maybe someone somewhere had wanted it and offered a great deal of money for it and it had been stolen and sold. It was probably out of the country while we slept. Then rumours started. Some people deduced that

25

because I had been, well, distracted, they figured maybe it was me and these things get round and a cloud hangs over a person, if you see what I mean.

Pitt Did you take it, Frank?

Frank I'm not a thief. I swear I'm not.

Pitt Good, Frank. Good. The corporate world frowns upon duplicity.
I need coffee. Then we'll continue.

Frank Could I get them?

Pitt Thank you, Frank. That's a demonstration of initiative. There's a franchise on Floor 17.

Frank exits.

Gray Can I say your behaviour is a little inappropriate?

Pitt I'm not displaying my genitals. For which we must be thankful.

Gray Advising the candidate to 'get the hell out'.

Pitt I like Frank. He's an original.

Gray You seem to be experiencing wild fluctuations of opinion.
Frank is a freak.

Pitt You chose him. Congratulations, a rare demonstration of flare.

Gray We don't want to encourage him in his freakiness. We want to run the interview as smoothly as possible.

Pitt It's like we're being watched.

Gray Watched?

Pitt Is there something I don't know? Are they letting people go?

Gray I think you're affected. I don't think you know you are, but you are.

Pitt Apart from my post-traumatic shock syndrome I'm completely normal.

Gray Are you doing anything for that?

Pitt What do you suggest?

Gray What does Sheila say?

Pitt Pills.

Gray Is that all?

Pitt She takes them.

Gray I don't think that's very professional.

Pitt You were always very down on Sheila.
   But you have to see it from her point of view. She's worked too long in Limehouse. Once a patient walked in with three penises in a Safeway bag and only one of them was his. She's had post-traumatic stress syndrome for years.
   She says take pills there's fuck else you can do.

Gray I'm sorry about what happened to you, I really am.

Pitt Is that why you never phoned?

Gray I phoned you twice.

Pitt Twice!

Gray You could have phoned me.

Pitt I was unconscious. I had three broken ribs, two fractured wrists and extensive bruising.

Gray Do we have to go through this now?

Pitt When else do I get to see you? Thank you for your text. I opened it with my nose.

27

Gray There's never a nice way to do these things. We need to focus.

Pitt Dumped by predictive text. Life always has new joys to throw in one's path.

Gray I'm sorry. You come back. In bandages. They project an image. I'm supposed to what? Ignore them? I'm doing a job here. They are signalling to me.

Pitt They're fucking bandages.

Gray They look theatrical.

Pitt You're all heart.

Gray Women grew up in the eighties. We don't have to be the heart and soul of this world any more. I'm not the kind of woman who likes her penises in a bag.
    Hello, Frank.

Frank has entered with bag of coffees.

Frank I mentioned your names. (*Frank distributes coffees.*) Decaffeinated organic semi-skimmed soya latte, no sugar. (*He gives it to Dr Gray.*)

Gray Thank you.

Frank Black. (*He gives it to Dr Pitt, and takes his own.*)

Gray We're going to put you on the spot, Frank.
    Imagine you're visiting a household for the first time. Your task is twofold; to discover whether this particular household is suitable for the case study in question and also to begin to refine your data-gathering questions.

Frank Fine. That's fine.

Pitt You think you could run a research programme? Refine the data-gathering schedule and collect the data?

Frank Sure, I would examine the internal coherence of the items in a sample of households using a statistical test of reliability such as Cronbach's Alpha. Alternatively a set of items may be grouped to form a Guttman Scale.

Pitt Right. Good, Frank.

Gray You have your scenario there? (*She indicates a slip of paper.*) Dr Pitt and I are members of the same household. Is everything clear?

Frank Yes. Can I go out and come in?

Pitt Sure.

Frank Just helps. I'm a little worried about this particular part of the interview.

Pitt Just relax, Frank.

Frank Role-play is a slightly intimidating concept.

Pitt There's nothing to worry about, really.

Frank I appreciate your support, Dr Pitt.

Pitt My pleasure, Frank.

Frank I realise I got off to a bad start with the bear.

Pitt Forget the bear.

Frank Of course a yoghurt has to be attractive. I wasn't looking at it from the right perspective.

Pitt Listen, we all had a laugh about the bear.

Frank You did?

Pitt Yeah. A kid could have come up with the idea in five seconds. Some overpaid executive came up with a bear in a sailor suit, holding a yoghurt and skipping.

Frank Did Dr Gray laugh about the bear, too?

Pitt She laughed the hardest.

Gray I refute any such suggestion.

Pitt Yeah, well, she's not going to admit it.

She's going to have you believe we sit here taking a bear holding a spoon seriously.

Frank Because a bear has big paws.

Pitt Exactly. You know what she called that bear, Frank?

Gray I did not.

Pitt Phyllis.

Frank Cute.

Pitt Yup. We'd make up little stories. How's Phyllis this morning? She has her period. She's given up on the Atkins diet. She feels let down by the lack of alternatives within the current political system.

Frank I feel a good deal more relaxed now, Dr Pitt.

Pitt Take your time. Frank.

Frank exits.

Gray What are you doing?

Pitt I was siding with the candidate, encouraging him.

Gray Are you trying to undermine me?

Pitt I was lightening the atmosphere.

Gray You were humiliating me. You have an aggressive goal. You're building some kind of bond with the interviewee, edging me out, leaving me vulnerable.

Pitt To what?

Gray We're a Band D household. Blue Collar workers. A town in Eastern Russia. Have you read the suggested responses?

Pitt It's not Chekhov, is it?

Gray Each interview segment is time-delimited within the fruit of the organic schedule.

Pitt Whose idea was that?

Gray Marcia's idea. It's a good idea.

Pitt Sounds like a salad. Oh, come on, where's your sense of humour?

Gray We need to provide him with an unseen obstacle. It's suggested that one of us is reluctant to answer his questions, maybe deeply suspicious.
     That could be you.

Pitt Me?

Gray We could play to type.

Pitt You're suggesting I have a suspicious nature?

Gray I just want to get through this. The camera, it's stressful.

Pitt Of course.

Gray But it's good if we can be civilised about this.

Pitt That's right.

Gray Because we need to separate work from personal agenda.

Pitt Definitely.

Gray Wonderful. We can negotiate the change-curve.

Pitt Absolutely. Is there someone else?

   Frank knocks at the door.

(*Calls.*) We need a little more time in here, Frank.

Gray Where do you get off asking a question like that?

Pitt Because I notice you've been avoiding me lately.

Gray It's like you haven't read *The Seven Habits of Highly Effective Operators*.

Pitt I never did. I'm not religious. Who was it you began to see when I was lying in bed all smashed up like mushy fruit?

Gray Oh, please.

Pitt Am I being a little dramatic?

Gray We were an item, what, a matter of months?

Pitt Six months.

Gray Is there a law against a single woman taking a lover? Who wrote that law? Show me. Let me put a gun to her temple.

Pitt Who is it?

Gray You're the one with a spouse at home to rattle pills with.

Pitt Is it someone I know?

Gray Come on in, Frank.

Frank enters.

Frank Good afternoon. Thank you so much for taking the time to see me. I appreciate it. (*He breaks from the role momentarily.*) Could we say this is the breakfast table?

They sit round.

Gray We're being paid for this, aren't we?

Frank Well, yes, yes, you are. But I still appreciate it.

Gray Because I've taken time off work and so has my mother.

Frank Well, thank you for that. And you will be reimbursed. The company is very prompt in these matters. Can I ask what is the work you do?

Gray I do hotel work. I used to be a cannery manager before it closed.

Frank And your mother?

Dr Pitt looks at her briefing paper.

Pitt I raise my own chickens.

Frank That must be very satisfying.

Pitt For the chickens, maybe.

Gray Have you any identification?

Frank I have a passport and a letter from the local police station. We leafleted the whole area.

Gray I'm just being cautious. If you knew my personal history, you'd understand.

Pitt My daughter once fell into a canning machine. It left her highly suspicious of strangers.

Frank That must have been a terrifying experience.

Gray I was referring to a recent event. I expect you know what happened here.

Frank Yes. (*He reads.*) The economic collapse of the former USSR devastated this region socially and economically.

Gray It ripped the heart out of our town.

Frank Yes. Would it be fair to say that since then you have re-evaluated your lives and priorities and consequently changed your behaviour patterns? Do you, for example, find yourself spending more time at home with family?

Gray Yes, we enjoy more family time together.

Frank How is that?

Pitt Suffocating.

Frank Will the new-found focus on family affect your holiday shopping habits during the Christmas period? I have a checklist here. Do you consider these gifts suitable, taking into account recent events? Yes, no or maybe?

While Dr Gray responds, Dr Pitt refuses.

Frank A family game.

Gray Yes.

Frank A lawnmower?

Gray Yes.

Frank A spun-glass ornament, say a deer or a woman in evening wear on horseback?

Gray Maybe.

Frank Soap on a rope?

Gray Maybe.

Frank A handkerchief monogrammed with the initials of a family member?

Gray Yes.

Frank A home entertainment system?

Gray Yes.

Frank An exotic beach holiday?

Gray No.

Frank A violent action toy?

Gray No.

Frank I noticed you're mother is not responding to the questions. Can I ask why?

Gray You can try.

Pitt The thing is, young man, you can ask my daughter all the questions in the world and she'll say whatever she has to, to look good.

Frank Are you saying you might answer differently?

Pitt What can I say? I would love a soap on a rope but I never got so much as a spit on a tissue. So you might as well tear up that piece of paper with your answers, 'cos it's all lies.

Frank Ah . . .

Gray My mother is a little unreliable. She's eighty-six.

Pitt I'm forty-six.

Gray Don't work yourself up, Mother.

Pitt Just between the two of us, my daughter is a hateful slut.
  It was my birthday last week. Guess what I got?

Frank Um – nothing much?

Pitt That's right. Big fat-arse zero, and do you know where I was?

Frank No.

Pitt Dying.

Frank Oh, dear.

Pitt Don't leave me with her.

Frank Whatever it is will blow over.

Pitt A whole personality doesn't blow over.

Frank Well, thank you, it's been a delight.

Gray Let's debrief. Can you conjecture as to why you aroused so much hostility, Frank?

Frank This is my first household, and I can see that there is a little tension, which isn't surprising considering what the community has gone through.

Gray Are there any strategies you might employ?

Frank There are obviously a lot of difficult emotions flying about. I wouldn't like them to think I felt superior in any way. I might tell a little story about my own family. For example, my father once shoved a potato up my mother's exhaust when she was trying to escape. When it shot out it was completely cooked.

Pitt He sounds perfect for my daughter.

Frank My mother pointed out she could have been killed.

Pitt The potato murderer.

Frank My father then tried to lighten the atmosphere by eating the potato.

Gray Even though we were members of the same family there are significant economic variables, but you cannot be expected to draw conclusions from the differing responses to the gifts because Dr Pitt didn't make any responses. (*to Dr Pitt*) That is taking an obstacle to a ludicrous extreme.

Pitt It's better for Frank to have a taste of what it's like.

Gray I don't think you can expect the company to agree with you.

Pitt I think they'll appreciate lateral thinking. Sometimes people don't want to answer your questions, Frank, even if you're paying them. They just want to get things off their chest, especially if they're old or drunk or women. And if they're all three, well, you're fucked.

Frank I can see that. (*He laughs.*)

Gray Frank, we're going to take a moment aside. (*She takes Dr Pitt aside.*) OK, you want to know.

Pitt Yes.

Gray Then will you conduct this interview in a less confrontational fashion?

Pitt Yes.

Gray It may floor you.

Pitt I've grown to appreciate the horizontal.

Gray It's Marcia.

Pitt Marcia! You couldn't have picked someone a little superior? What were you trying to do, knock my confidence?

Gray Say what you like. Nothing sticks to Marcia. She's immune to unsuccessful feedback.

Pitt Fucking Marcia!

Dr Gray re-addresses Frank.

Gray Frank, in retrospect, were there any further questions you'd have for the Russian household?

Frank I do need to make a final assessment as to whether this family is suitable for inclusion in the wider study. It would be helpful for me to know to what extent the breakdown in familial relations is due to recent history because that would affect my assessment of the data. Is this family representative or is it nuts?

Pitt Are you happy wading in there with that kind of question, Frank?

Frank Um, yeah.

Gray It needs to be phrased a little more carefully.

Pitt It is possible that you will arouse some hostility.
   If mother was a little sprightlier she might set about you with a handy farming implement.

Frank Does that kind of thing happen?

Gray No. You are protected by certain boundaries.

Pitt These people never leave the building. Mentally their outlook is monolithic.
   Anthropologists should stick together.

Frank Are you saying there's a split in the company?

Gray That is a misrepresentation.

Frank As a future employee, it doesn't inspire confidence.

Gray I agree with Frank. Your assertions are slanderous, Dr Pitt.

Pitt We have to go to these places, we get our hands dirty.

Gray How is staying in a hotel and running a team of local anthropologists getting your hands dirty?

Pitt When you're face to face with people, Frank, sometimes things aren't so clear-cut, that's all I'm saying. I mean, maybe Mother wouldn't answer your questions because she thinks they are inane. She has a point.

Gray You wouldn't answer the questions, Dr Pitt, let's be clear about this.

Pitt I know what I'm talking about. I have an affinity with other living creatures.
   You skipped that gene.

Gray I'm sure you don't mind me reiterating that a tendency to over-personalise needs to be avoided.

Pitt Don't you think Dr Gray has an inhuman quality?

Frank Um.

Gray Listen, I'm sorry I forgot your birthday. Get over it.

Pitt Look at her.
 Her eyes. Like a kind of evil fish. These are the people we have to work with.

Gray May I remind you we are in the process of an interview?

Pitt A heartless evil fish.
 You got to ask yourself what kind of set-up is this? See this? (*Shows bandages.*)

Frank You were hit during an interview situation?

Gray That's misleading. She incurred those in her leisure time.

Pitt I had an accident, Frank, and for a bit all I wanted was the pain to stop. And then I wanted to feel like I used to feel, but that was somehow unavailable to me. Then I realised I only knew what I wanted when something was taken away. And that's what our job is. To find what has been taken away and plug the gap with something else that pretends to be the answer.

Gray The company has a record of scrupulous good practice.

Pitt Soap on a fucking rope, Frank.

Gray May I remind you that the company wishes to provide each candidate with a quasi-identical interview within the overall simultaneity of the process.

Pitt Why are you acting for the camera?

Gray I just want to complete this interview to the best of my ability for the candidate's sake.

Pitt She's even using her best side. I mean what is this, an audition?

 Beat.

What do you think to our centrepiece, Frank?

Frank Off the record? It's OK. What is it?

Pitt I don't know. Sell it to me.

Frank Now?

Pitt Go ahead.

Frank It's round, it's art and it's heavy, so you can't knock it off the table. Every civilisation has pursued art. What for? Who knows, but maybe it's a good idea not to stop. We know instinctively that it enriches our lives. Imagine if everyone had the same curtains. We would feel that we were living in an Orwellian nightmare. So here we have a round thing but it is also egg-like, suggesting eggs and all things associated with eggs, and it's yours for three hundred pounds.

Pitt We've been bought. Is that right?

 Beat.

Like you said, this is a new carpet. Who put it there, Dr Gray?

Gray Is this relevant to the interview?

Pitt This is a lesson, Frank. How come you never see things that are staring you in the face?

Frank Is that a question you want me to answer?

Pitt There is no answer.

Frank Maybe I should just stand over here? (*He goes and stands at a little distance.*)

Pitt Who bought us?

Gray A new company. They bought us and soon they're going to sell us.
   There's no need to panic, it may hardly affect us.

Pitt Sell us?

Gray When they've improved our total organisational performance and marketability. That's what they do.

Pitt That's parasitic.

Gray Try looking at it from their perspective. Don't be defensive and blaming.

Pitt So they are rationalising.

Gray They are looking to eliminate functions, to trim the fat off.
   The first duty of a company is to survive.
   Would it have helped if I'd told you? You were demonstrating a paranoid sensibility.

Pitt Are you surprised? So what's the orb for?

Gray It has a frictionless surface. It promotes harmony and strengthens the immune system.

Pitt What a fucking joke. You set me up and then you stood by and watched me assassinate myself.

At this point Dr Pitt stumbles forward. She appears to be warding off punches. She falls to the floor. Writhes as if being kicked.

Frank Dr Pitt . . .

Gray Jacqueline? At this point in the proceedings Dr Pitt became temporarily indisposed.

Dr Gray switches off the camera.

Oh, God.

Dr Pitt is shaking still. She cries out suddenly and throws her arm over her face. Suddenly she realises where she is.

Are you OK?
(*to Frank*) Could you get some water, please?

Frank Sure. (*He goes to pour some from bottle to cup.*)

Frank Dr Pitt? Here, drink this. (*Offers cup.*)

Frank You had a kind of fit.

Pitt Yeah. I have them occasionally.

Frank Are you sick?

Pitt Just let me lie here a minute.

Gray You just take a moment.

Pitt I have these fits, sometimes. But they say they're going to go.

Frank Yes?

Pitt Since the accident.

Frank Oh, right.

Pitt It's like I'm getting hurt all over again.

Frank Do you want a hug?

Pitt No.

Gray Are you all right?

Pitt Yes.

Gray goes and lights a cigarette. Smokes.

Frank Can I tell you something?

Pitt It's not going to freak me out, is it? I've been on your side till, now, Frank.

Frank That was amazing.

Pitt It is going to freak me out.

Frank Do you believe in synchronicity?

Pitt No.

Frank I've seen these films.

Pitt That's too general a premise to support a theory of synchronicity, Frank.

Frank For my final piece of research, on Siberian shamans.

Pitt I have a headache.

Frank I saw these films of shamans, and they have these kind of fits.
  Just like you. They even shout like you shouted.

Pitt Yeah?

Frank They go into altered states in order to perform healing ceremonies.

Pitt I know what a shaman is, Frank.

Frank But the weird thing is that each shaman has an animal, like a witch had a familiar, to guide it into the spirit world and ensure safe return. Very commonly that was a bird, a water bird.

Pitt Yeah?

Frank Yeah.

Pitt Excuse me.

Gray Yes, you take a break.

  Dr Pitt exits.

Frank Poor Dr Pitt.
  It was pretty nasty seeing her writhing on the ground like that.

Gray It was a very convenient fit.

Frank You mean . . . it was a very convenient fit?

Gray You know what just happened there, Frank? She saved herself.

Frank She did?

Gray Dr Pitt has been conducting herself in an unorthodox manner, to say the least. Now she has provided an excuse for her conduct. The company will feel uneasy about reprimanding her.

Frank They have a point.

Gray She has continually sabotaged your interview. Why has she done that? Because she fears you, fears for her job, and so she is jeopardising yours.

Frank I feel a little sorry for her.

Gray Crush that instinct. Do you want her to make you look ineffectual? Lose the career you have a right to? This is important to you, isn't it, Frank?

Frank This is my chance.

Gray Yes. So what I'm asking you to do, Frank, is to make a complaint.

Frank A complaint?

Gray The next time Dr Pitt responds in an inappropriate manner, challenge her. Speak your concerns aloud. To the camera.

Frank I don't know if I can do that.

Gray We need you to weigh in against her, Frank. Your complaint would tip the balance.

Beat.

There is a thing in business called burn-out.

44

Frank I've heard of it.

Gray Some people work for a long time extremely well, they may even have an exceptional reputation in their field, and then one day it's as if the spark that charges them is extinguished and then it's better for them and for everyone that they stop. And that's what's happened to Dr Pitt. She's destroying her good name. She needs to be stopped. You would be doing her a favour.

Frank I don't know if she would see it like that.
  Maybe she needs help.

Gray There are some circumstances where you can't help people, Frank. I'm a woman, I should know. Some women stay with men their whole lives trying to 'help' them; because they're slobs, they're alcoholics, they don't mean to hit them. But you know what I'd tell those women – get the hell out. Isn't that right?

Frank Well, yeah.

Gray I mean stay, if you want the lifeblood sucked out of you, if you want your teeth smashed to bits. You know what I'd say to a woman who was loyal to a man like that?

Frank What?

Gray You deserved it. You should've cut the cord. It's only a little blood, compared to a lifetime's. Do not imagine that people are weak and need help, Frank. That is a disabling fantasy. That makes us feel better. It makes us less afraid.
  When you are guilty, Frank, you are not an effective action taker. You have to imagine that Dr Pitt is a rhino.

Frank I think I'll find that a little difficult.

Gray All that 'will' and power focused on the main chance and with a hide of rocky leather. That is much more what people are like and you have to start imagining them all as rhinos.

Frank That's quite a lot of work. For example, babies.

Gray Whatever. The point is that if you don't brace yourself for a fight with a rhino, what will happen?

Frank I don't honestly think if a rhino was in this room, Dr Gray, there'd be much we could do except maybe pray that it had some kind of lethargic disease.

Gray That is superstition, Frank. Have you read a book *The Seven Habits of Highly Effective Operators*?

Frank No.

Gray Put it on your list. There is always something to do.

Frank I suppose maybe if I had a stun gun or some rhino food . . .

Gray That is the way to think.

Frank Is this part of the interview?

Gray What?

Frank What you just said – is it all part if it?

Gray Well, that's up to you to work out.

Frank The thing is, I like Dr Pitt.

Gray Frank. Dr Pitt and I were good friends. She helped me, you know, when I started here. But that does not mean that I am prepared to fail my organisation.
  I am strong enough to see what I have to do? Are you?

Frank This is tough.

Gray What do you think is on offer here? We have landed a big new client, the biggest. Oil. This affects our consequent restructuring. Now, if the company likes you, if you succeed, you can progress along an escalator of achievement, each stage with sufficient executive remuneration. Wouldn't you like to earn enough to retire at forty, Frank?

Frank Forty!

Gray At thirty-five?

Frank God.

Gray Thirty-two? You could have a new second career that meant something? You could dig where you liked. You'd never have to see the inside of an office again.

Frank Wow.

Gray When she walks back in here she will be looking to save herself in any way she can. A wounded animal is dangerous. Survival is premium. They will lash out. You have to be prepared.

Frank So it's me or Dr Pitt.

Gray Your job or hers.

Frank That's kind of primitive. You'd have thought things would have advanced a little in the third millennium.

Gray Don't give me any anthropological shit. This is a fight to the death.

Dr Pitt re-enters.

How are you feeling?

Pitt I'd like this on camera, please.

Dr Gray switches on the camera.

I apologise. I've been behaving erratically.
This is a common pattern of behaviour for people who've survived a trauma.

It leads to an 'episode'. I feel sure that now I can proceed without incident. I have a long and distinguished record of work with the company. This episode is anomalous. I hope, Frank, that you'll excuse me.

Frank I'd certainly appreciate it if you could go ahead and interview me in as normal fashion as you can possibly manage.

Pitt Certainly, Frank. It would be my pleasure.

Frank I can't believe every candidate is having the same interview I am.

Pitt Who knows, maybe my insanity will work to your advantage.

Gray For the record I would like it to be known that the interview has not adhered strictly to the specified times due to the above-mentioned interruptions.
    I'm glad we cleared the air.

Pitt I can clear the air, the room, a life. It's surprisingly easy to achieve.

Frank I'm not sure you should be giving me these kind of details, Doctor.

Pitt You're right.

Frank I mean, I feel I have to be a little tough here.

Pitt Yeah? Why's that, Frank?

Frank No particular reason.

   Beat.

Except, well, I read a book. *The Seven Habits of Highly Effective Operators*.
   And it said I had to be effective and tough.

   Beat.

48

Pitt Let's continue. The camera is rolling. (*She switches on the camera.*) We are now going to consider the art of teamwork, Frank.
   Any thoughts?

Gray This is a deviation from the rubric.

Pitt Frank?

Frank Let me see. A team is a set of persons working or playing in combination in order to make a co-operative effort.

Pitt That's the definition.

Frank And I can see that kind of makes sense. If you want to do something like, say, building a building.

Pitt Or participating in an interview.

Frank Yes.

Pitt People need to work together to achieve a goal.

Frank The goal is important.

Pitt And how might it fall apart, Frank?

Frank Fall apart? Why would it fall apart?

Pitt I'm asking the questions.

Frank The goals, if the goals were not the same goals. Or if people didn't see the goals they had as the same goals as the other people's goals.

Pitt That's too many goals in one sentence, Frank.
   Give me an example. Let's stick with the interview scenario.

Gray Isn't that a little close to home?

Pitt Let's imagine we had different objectives in this room.

49

Frank Do we have to?

Pitt Would you agree there would have to be two types of players? Allies and enemies?

Frank Isn't there a somewhere-in-the -middle type of person?

Pitt A loser, Frank. So which type are you?

Frank An ally, I suppose.

Pitt Whose ally, Frank? Mine, or Dr Gray's.

Gray I'm not sure about this line of questioning.

Pitt Well, Frank?

Frank Maybe we have different goals.

Pitt Me and you, Frank?

Frank Because I want this job and maybe you don't want me to have it.

Pitt Frank. I know on the face of it you're not the housewife's choice, you're eccentric, lateral and occasionally insulting, but appearances can be deceiving and my instincts tell me, yes, I'm for you.

Frank Thank you. I'm confused.

Gray Frank. Don't be bullied.

Pitt I'm not bullying you, Frank, I'm just saying that there are politics in every situation and you have to be clear about what you're being recruited to.

Frank But what if two people are trying to recruit you to different things and you're in an interview and you can't afford to alienate either side? Like there's a fork in the road and on one path a maiden is beckoning you and on the other, there you stand, Dr Pitt, scratching your hoof in the dust and snorting.

Pitt I've never done that in my life, mainly because I'm not an ungulate.

Frank It's like I can't win. It's ridiculous. Wait. Did you arrange this between you before?

Pitt Arrange what, Frank?

Gray You don't have to answer that question.

Frank I get it. Dr Gray and yourself are a 'team'. And yet you have continually acted in ways which contradict your team-ship. You do not have shared goals.

Gray That's a very interesting manner of reply, Frank. Turning the camera on us, so to speak. Perhaps you could refer to your own experiences.

Frank Furthermore, you have, and I am quoting, each in some sense enlisted me against the other.

Pitt Enlisted?

Frank And if I was unfamiliar with the rigours of team-ship I would have fallen for this. But I am fully aware of your ploy and I refute it entirely.

Pitt So you had a little talk?

Frank This was not a real conversation. It was a fake attempt to turn me against you, which I saw through.

Pitt Go on.

Frank The escalators of achievement, executive remunerations. These things are not mutually exclusive. I can still want them and work in a team. Please ask me another question.

Pitt No, Frank, I would like to unpick this one a little.

Gray This is not pertinent to the interview. I'm switching off the camera.

It is nineteen hundred hours.

I don't think you knew about the executive remunerations, Jacqueline.

Pitt I knew jack-shit about them.

Executive remunerations are paid to survivors, Frank.
Some people have to die first. People like me who have
been working their cunts dry and don't deserve the knife
slipping in but they get it. You came to a decision with
my colleague, to what? Eliminate me?

Frank Well – we didn't say it like that. This was not
'real'.

Pitt I'm disappointed, Frank, really. I liked you.

Frank I like you, Dr Pitt.

Pitt You know what happened here, Frank. You were
corrupted.

Frank Jesus. I wasn't easy to persuade, if that's what you
think.

Pitt I'd call five minutes pretty fucking fast.

Frank I felt sorry for you.

Pitt I should have added 'gullible' to my list.

Frank I feel bad. You're in bandages and everything.

Gray She had an accident. So what? That does not give
her moral superiority. We could step out into the traffic
any time we chose. Everybody plays to win. She comes
back like she's had an epiphany. Give her a week and
she'll be no different. This is a lesson, Frank, it's what
we all do.

Pitt It wasn't an accident.

You're in a hotel room, Frank, somewhere in Russia.
It's a boom town now, where the executives hang out.

There's a knock on the door – who walks in . . .?

Frank I don't know.

Pitt A woman, maybe thirty years old. She looks about, then she realises there's been a mistake. Obviously I didn't order any sex. She demands a Coke. Why not? What else do we have in common? Before I can give it to her she sits on the bed and slumps over. I call security. He arrives. He apologises. It's terrible, but there has been a lot of this recently. Girls pay staff to let them into the rooms to pleasure the guests. Maybe because my title is Doctor there's been a mistake. There certainly has. Can't you put a stop to it? I ask. Where to start? There is a demand. People are away from home. Ten dollars is cheap. This is a woman with two children to feed and her husband was killed in the war. That's terrible, I say, but it's two a.m. and I'd like to get some sleep. Do I travel a lot? he asks, and I smell that he's been drinking. I can smell that. Can you get her out? I say. But he has to file some kind of report of the incident, so maybe if I just want to sleep I should pay him the ten dollars and we can just forget it. But something in my head says to me that this is a *set-up* because I recognise the woman now – I fucking interviewed her and her mother, and the whole story is a lie and I still have my *pride*, and so I go ahead and say this doesn't make sense, and he looks at me like I don't make sense. This is a set-up, I say again – I'm not some fucking sap, some western sap you can piss all over.

This makes him very angry. Are you calling me a pimp? he says. Now I notice his eyes are red and mean. What am I accusing him of, he rages. And then he goes on, do I think he likes working here licking assholes? Bringing them women they haven't even got the guts to fuck? He comes up close to me: they come to our country, sneer at our women, slobber over our food, soft with dollars, eyes like babies. You think I earn a living here? It is impossible for a human being to live on what I earn, to provide for a family, etc., we have to sell our women to cunts. And then he lands the first punch which takes all the breath out of my body and I crumple like an old whore. And he kicks me in the side of the head. In a bit the woman comes over to look and I can't see her clearly because there's blood in my eyes and then I'm out cold.

Frank Now I don't feel bad. I feel terrible.

Pitt It's wild out there. They hate us. But it didn't kill me, Frank. It was when my lover deserted me; that's what killed me. Like watching your tribe walk away from you over the rim of the earth. The last stragglers don't turn back because it's unlucky. The last human beings you'll ever see.

Frank This is some interview.

Pitt What does this mean, Frank?

Frank I don't know.

Pitt Outside, just now, I figured something out. What happened; it means I'm immune. It means the company won't let me go because I have something on them. I'm special to them now. You should have stuck with me, Frank.

Frank If this is a test, I think I'm failing.

Gray We were never really together. You were with her.

Frank Are you starting as well, Doctor?

Gray Joined at the fucking hip/brain/whatever/cunt.

Frank I think you are. I would like to make a complaint now.

Gray Shut up, Frank.

Frank I think you're both getting a little emotional.

Pitt Tidal, Frank, this is a tsunami.

Frank I know what I have to do. I have to tell the company that it can't let things like that happen. It has to bring people along with them. It has to be good. This is why you need new people. We will change things. I can see now. I can see what you want and I'm telling you. I'm your man.

Is that what you wanted me to say?

Beat.

Shall I grab some more refreshments?

He exits.
Beat.

Pitt He can't keep getting the coffees.

Gray What does it matter now? I have seven minutes of interview. Marcia will have made a film by now. She was an actress, she has a flair for this kind of thing. She'll get a fucking BAFTA. It looks like I can't even run an interview. I just told our candidate to shut up. I blew up in the middle of a segment. I'll be out.

Pitt You want my sympathy? You enlisted the candidate against me.

Gray Because I knew it would be war. When you found out I didn't tell you we'd been financially acquired.

Pitt You knew that we're rationalising and you wanted it to be me, not you.

Gray That makes it sound grubby.

Pitt It is grubby.
You, Marcia, the escalators, and I was out?

Gray The thing is, I know it looks bad – the timing. This is what I want to say to you. When I started seeing Marcia, it was a coincidence, if you like. I'm sorry.

Pitt A coincidence?

Gray Yes. You were sick.

In this place you need someone to watch your back for you.

Pitt You didn't wait around long.

Gray They already started. I came back from lunch. The desk next to me was empty. Marco didn't even get to clear it himself. They put his stuff in a box and threw it in the lift. He had to collect it round the back. For a while he was outside. We couldn't hear what he was saying but he was waving his arms about. I still have his sharpener. I don't understand what he did. I felt pretty sick.

Pitt What did you do?

Gray What could we do? Sign a petition? Continuous restructuring is the future. It happened. It was necessary. I didn't even like Marco. Marcia didn't do anything and she's been fucking him for years.

Pitt Marco is married with three kids.

Gray Why else would he fuck Marcia? This is all I have. My job. How many people would like to be in my place? Three hundred? Three thousand? Now, maybe, I'm going to lose it. So, I'm scared – is that a sin? We're all scared.

Marco is driving a taxi.

Pitt No?

Gray He was jacked by two fourteen-year-old crackheads in Hackney. They wrote off his car.

Pitt Christ.

Gray Now he's scared to leave the house.

Pitt Are you asking me to help you? Do you think I'm some kind of masochistic recidivist?

Gray I was hoping.

Beat.

So you're going to let me, what, sink? If you'd have made a decision we'd be in it together.

Pitt I was in the process of leaving.

Gray You were way off schedule.

Pitt What did you want me to do? Put her stuff in a box? I was about to tell her that very day.

Beat.

Gray What happened to you? Even before you were beaten up everybody noticed a kind of falling away – your performance indicators. That's when I first started talking to Marcia. What's happening to her? Marcia said it's like she's switched off.

Pitt What happened? I met you, I fell down a hole.

Gray Did it really hurt?

Pitt That was a metaphor.

Gray In the hotel?

Pitt What do you want me to say? I sleep with the light on: if I sleep.

Gray You do?

Pitt You're skirting close to a stereotype: business people have no imagination.

Gray This bad thing happened to you. It's holding you back. Now I understand.

I think you have to think about it in terms of goal-setting within everyday activities.

Let's start with the bandages. Let me help you with those. (*She indicates bandages.*)

Pitt No.

Gray Do you know why you're wearing bandages?
You're hoping they will hold you together.

Pitt Is there even an entry under 'bandages'? You could
live your whole life in that book.

Gray Got any better ideas?

Beat.

What I want to know is, what kind of woman leaves her
hotel door open?

Pitt What?

Gray A woman looks over her shoulder her whole life.
It's like inviting something in to destroy you. Like some
part of your psyche was faulty, porous, and it let in
something destructive.

Pitt What are you saying, it was my fault?

Gray Well, what were you thinking?

Pitt I was thinking of you. I was happy, trusting. Before
you I didn't want to wake up in the mornings.

Gray That means we don't have to lose.

Pitt Don't try to work me.

Gray You're not immune. No one is. Marco said he was
going to sell his story. He was going to do something.
People cannot be treated in this way. His stuff went the
wrong way in the lift and he never got it back.

He had some dirt on the company. No paper would
touch it. Nobody cares.

So what? A pimp beat you up. It happens. The company
has clean hands.

Plus he suspects the carjack was a set up. To warn him
off. Maybe he's paranoid . . . So what are we going to

do? You know what Frank has on us? That we had some emotional meltdown.

Two women who are lovers. That is a story. I wouldn't want that getting round.

Pitt He doesn't think like that.

Gray He comes over as a fool, but maybe, you know, he's cleverer that he looks. And he has beguiled us into letting down our masks And now he has leverage. He has us.

Beat.

You think I liked it you changed? I looked round. Where were you?

Dr Gray helps Dr Pitt begin to take off bandages.

These come off easily. Doesn't hurt, does it? Our candidate is seriously socially challenged, plus he short-circuits on presentation and general morality. Plus he's junked the ethos of the company.

We could say that together.

We could do it together. We could win.

Beat.

Most people give up just when they are about to achieve success – one foot from a winning touch. Failure is not the falling down but the staying down.

The bandages are off.

Feels better, doesn't it? (*She looks at arm.*) Looks naked.

Pitt It's a long time since it's seen the light of day.

Frank knocks.

Gray Look at you. You look just like before.

Are we agreed?

Frank knocks.

We're in it together?

Frank knocks.

Pitt Agreed.

Gray Come in.

Frank enters, puts down coffees.
Dr Gray switches on the camera.

Frank, part of what we need to achieve here today is what
we call a personality fit. You're obviously academically
an achiever, but would you enjoy the work? Does your
profile fit the profile? We need to make an assessment. Do
you have any questions?

Frank I think it does. Fit the profile.

Gray Can you be more specific?

Frank I sense a bit of trouble here. Can I be open about
this? If there's one aspect of my life that has been a little
troublesome, it would be my personality.

Gray Really?

Frank I'm not a very likeable person. I can talk to people
and then I run out of things to say. That must be my fault
because I'm not curious enough about them, but then
people aren't really curious about me either. But then
I put this down to the kind of lives we all lead.
  Separate lives. Lives which militate against curiosity
because intimacy and curiosity go together. Indigenous
peoples in the Siberian taiga where temperatures would
drop to minus 160 degrees would cram into the same tent
in order to generate warmth. Apparently it became so hot
they had to remove the garments from their upper bodies.
I imagine it was a little stuffy but never lonely, and also
very interesting and arousing, and I don't just mean in
the sexual department. In fact, that's very intriguing. Our
obsession with sex may arise from the anxiety that we
don't feel curious enough, aroused enough by others.

Pitt This is what I think we're trying to get at, Frank.

You will be a representative of our company – going into houses, interviewing.

You have to be reliable. Your mind tends to wander.

Frank But it wouldn't wander in the wrong circumstances.

I want to work in Russia.

Gray To be with your girlfriend, we understand.

Frank She's not actually my girlfriend. But I hope she will be.

Her archive on shamanic implements has to be seen to be believed.

Gray I don't doubt it. Well, you've told us a lot there, Frank.

Frank But I haven't given a good impression, have I? You think I'm coming over badly – you should see how much I've improved. I never spoke till I was five years old. My first word was 'spaghetti'.

You can imagine, my parents were beside themselves. I seemed to demonstrate early signs of autism. But then I grew out of it – mostly, although my mother is still suspicious.

Pitt Frank, if you didn't get this, it wouldn't be the end of the world.

It'll only seem like it. You're young. There'll be other avenues.

Frank You're speaking like you know I'm not going to get it.

Pitt Not at all, the decision doesn't rest with us alone.

I'm just flagging up the possibility, Frank.

Frank I can understand you're angry with me, Dr Pitt, and I deeply regret past misunderstandings.

But I can make it up to you.

Pitt You spoke to us earlier about the company, Frank. You said it to had to change. That in some way it was not good. Do you want to say a little more about that?

Frank I can see what you're trying to do.
   Can we switch off the tape?

Gray We need to make up time, Frank.

Frank I really need it to be off for a minute, that's all.

   Dr Gray switches off the tape.
      Frank takes something out of his pocket and holds out his hand.

Pitt What's that?

Frank It's a bird, only 13.7 cm in diameter. The tail is broken off approximately four centimetres from the tip, but the head is quite perfect. It's certainly a shamanic property.

Pitt You took that?

Frank I was there when it was found.

Pitt That is a priceless object.

Frank Yes.

Pitt And you stole it.

Gray That's a criminal act.

Frank I know.

Pitt Jesus, Frank, it's a denial on a global scale.
   Everyone has the right to experience the existence of that bird. That is our heritage.

Frank I feel bad, honestly I do.

Pitt You feel bad? You have stolen from every single person on this planet and every single human being to come.

Frank OK, you don't have to rub it in.

Pitt Fucking hell, Frank. You have to give it back.

Frank I want to give it back but it's hard. I could go to prison. I'd never work in the field again. So I'm thinking of a way.

Pitt Whatever possessed you, Frank?

Frank I didn't set out to steal it. I just wanted to borrow it. Then I was going to put it back. But when I held it I felt a different thing, that I had picked up a thread that had been lost, a thread that connected me back to something, where people made beautiful things that had powerful meanings. And once that thought came into my mind I knew I was not going to give it up. That somehow if I kept hold of it, it would be my guide just like it had been a guide thirty thousand years ago. You want to hold it, Doctor?

Pitt I don't want to be involved.

Frank It was a sacred object.

Gray I think we must agree to terminate this interview. Do you agree, Jacqueline?

Frank No, you can't do that.

Gray Because I feel the candidate has demonstrated serious unsuitability.

Frank I showed it to you because when I return it, which I intend to, I will not be a trusted member of the society of field-working anthropologists. I wanted to prove to you how much I need this job.

Pitt You've done this thing, Frank. It's hard to overlook.

Frank It chose me, that's what you have to understand.
   The spontaneous vocation of the shaman may begin with the shaman becoming extremely nervous and withdrawn.

That's what happened to me. I was wandering about like a lunatic. The totem will make you feel strongly attracted to it. What else would have impelled me to steal it?

Pitt So what are you saying? That you're what? A shaman?

Frank I know how it sounds. I've been experimenting with altered states.

Pitt We all take recreational drugs, Frank.

Frank I want to make amends.
The sacred object is placed before the supplicant.

He puts the bird on the ground before Dr Pitt. He then sits next to it.
Frank takes out a joint.

Pitt What's that?

Frank Blow.

Gray Marijuana. Jesus. There's not even a box to tick.

Frank lights up.

Frank The power object must be bathed in holy smoke.

Pitt How would we explain that our candidate was blowing Moroccan over a purloined artefact of considerable historic significance? It doesn't sound good.

Gray Shall I call security?

Pitt Be reasonable, Frank. We don't want to ruin your life.

Gray Leave him to it. It's over anyway. (*She sits, writes on her notes.*)

Frank The workmanship on these animals, the delicacy and precision, is something that defies historic logic. It supersedes the art that follows it until maybe the late Mayan period or the Egyptian tomb paintings. That subverts our notion of human development. The complex concept these people had of the universe is arguably as intricate as ours, which is fundamentally buying and selling.

You have to ask a question.

Pitt I do?

Frank Sure. This is for you. Do you have a question?

Pitt No.

Frank I think you do, about your soul.
You've been sick. That is a sign that it's lost.

Pitt Yeah?

Frank I'm going to help you get it back.

Pitt That's very kind, but it won't affect the outcome of your interview.

Frank I shall journey out with my spirit guide to look for any of your soul parts that are ready and willing to come home.
I am a technician of ecstasy.

Frank offers Dr Pitt the joint. Dr Pitt takes it.

Gray Are you taking that stuff? Is that advisable?

Pitt I'm having a bad day.

Frank Through ecstasy one encounters an alternate reality, which these people expertly developed via the use of experimental drugs. When they came back down to earth, returned – what would there be? – the comfort of knowing the world is not a prison. Usually there'd be some drumming or whatever.

Pitt We wouldn't want Marcia running in here.

Dr Pitt passes back joint.

Frank I'm focusing on the bird. (*He blows smoke onto it. He feels the hit.*) Wow. I'm flying.

Gray Maybe it's spiked.

Frank Look at you. You're kind of glowing.

Frank passes the joint to Dr Pitt.

I have to go into a cave.
I've never had to go into a cave before. It looks dark. I'm scared.

Pitt Frank?

She waves her hand in front of his eyes. He can't see.

Where did you score this stuff, Frank? It's lethal.

Frank I have a friend who does prison work.

Pitt Maybe you should come back now?

Frank Something's coming. (*Frank gives a cry.*) There's a sound. The beating of wings, hundreds. (*He gives another cry.*)

Gray What's happening?

Frank collapses on the floor and writhes in agony.

This is just great.

Frank goes still.

How was your day, Marcia? Oh, fine.
How was yours? Tremendous, our candidate is dead.

Pitt Frank? Frank?

Frank wakes up.

Frank I have your soul, Doctor.

Pitt Well, that's good news.

Frank I swallowed it.

Pitt I don't know how I feel about that, Frank.

Frank But I can regurgitate it.

Pitt Keep it, Frank.

Frank It sounds weird, but I just have to blow it back into your body.

Pitt Fuck off, Frank.

Frank It won't take a minute.

Gray Leave it, Frank.

Frank I have to. I can't walk around with two souls.

> *Frank lunges at Dr Pitt and 'blows' her soul back in. Dr Pitt punches Frank, who stumbles back and falls on the floor.*

Frank You hit me?

Pitt I was provoked.

Frank I was just trying to help.

Pitt You were sucking my back. That's not recognised interview protocol.

Gray This is out of control.

Frank You punched me. I was trying to save you.

Pitt Can I inform you of something? You performed your curative ritual inappropriately. The client, in such circumstances, doesn't partake of the mind-expanding substance. That is the prerogative of the shaman alone.
   What were you expecting? Some kind of transformation? That, Frank, is a fucking fairy tale. This is it. This room, these lights, this carpet. There's nothing else.

Frank You hit me. I demand the right to complete my interview.

Otherwise I go out there now and show someone what you did.

> *Beat.*
>> *Dr Pitt switches the camera on.*

Pitt Frank, the camera is on.

> *Dr Gray hands him some notes.*

We've reached our final section.

Let me explain that it reflects a different aspect of the work you may be required to partake in.

Frank I understand.

Pitt Look over the documents in front of you. Would you like to comment on them?

Frank They're minutes of a public meeting. (*He reads on.*)

Gray What's your impression?

Frank There's a conflict between the community and the company in question.

I would say that the community is demonstrating a fair level of anxiety.

Gray I would agree with that, but I would say the community is considerably less concerned than before the liaison took place.

There are a lot of pressures upon companies to be seen to be listening to the citizens of the environments they are developing. Since Russia's markets opened up there are many transnational companies working there and they have to satisfy their own investors as well as indigenous people as to their integrity. This is an area of work opening up for us. The land is presently so undeveloped as almost to be pristine.

Frank I was lost in this forest. It is beautiful.

Pitt People are concerned that these foreign firms, the kind that won't shit on their own doorstep, are going to be tempted to a place were they have no intrinsic loyalty or accountability. Very little protective legislation survived '89.

Frank It's kind of worrying when they talk about the sludge.

Pitt Yeah?

Frank (*reads*) Page two, paragraph seven: 'liquid wastes looking like cement dumped by a river'.

Gray These concerns were raised during a public question-and-answer session.
  Can you speculate on what our role might be?

Frank No company would want to face the music without knowing the ballpark area of questions. That would be our job: to know the questions in advance and inform the company. The areas of concern seem to be employment, gasification and ecological concerns, the benefits versus the drawbacks.

Gray That balance as it turned out was vital in managing community response to the project.

Frank Yeah. I can see that. People like to feel they're being listened to.

Pitt What are the areas of particular sensitivity?

Frank Sensitivity? Well. The lorries, carrying the pipes. They go too close to the schools. Yeah. I can see no one would like that particularly.

Pitt You would be happy to stay neutral on such issues? Because it's only fair to say it's an issue for us. We need to stay objective. We can't afford to be involved with these people.

Frank Yes, I see that.

Pitt Don't you have a particular affection for this part of the world, Frank?

Frank Yes.

Pitt Could you comment on the poisoned fish washed up in Piltun Bay? The construction works that are blocking the roads to the wild berry fields and fishing areas?

Frank I haven't read that far.

Pitt I'm telling you, Frank.

Frank Well, I would hope, I would hope, that these would be dealt with in a caring fashion.

Pitt We don't know that. We don't stay around long enough to find out.
   Bulldozers are ripping up the beaches of the bay. Habitats are destroyed, animals are fleeing. A guy woke up to find a bear in his hotel bedroom. And you think you can remain disinterested?

Frank I am a very calm person, Doctor. I have practised shamanic breathing techniques.

Pitt You're going to need them, Frank. Turn to page twenty-three.

Frank Page twenty-three?

Pitt The oil pipes are being laid over a fault line. There's been no extra investment in firefighting equipment. The pipeline may not withstand the serious earthquakes that hit the region. Forest fires are now more likely in any case from spills.
   What exactly are the long-term benefits when the oil runs out in twenty years and the forest is destroyed? Most of the profits go out of the country. What exactly are the benefits, Frank?

Frank Employment was just as high on the agenda as other matters.

Pitt I should think your forest will end up as rusting, rancid scorched earth.

Frank I'd like to put it on record that I don't appreciate the kind of bating that you have subjected me to during this interview. Earlier you also punched me in the plexus.

Pitt It does seem as if the benefits go all one way.

Frank It isn't fair, that you try to destroy my chances.

Gray You did a fair bit on your own, Frank.

Frank I want this.

Pitt You're a good person, Frank. You have this love for your subject You need to be researching the first use of the human fork. That would make you happy, Frank, believe me.

Frank You're wrong. You're testing me.

Pitt Look on the bright side. You don't want to turn out like me. I'm shaking, sweating. I wake up in the night shouting. I have flashbacks. I see a boot kicking my face. I still feel the blood in my mouth, thinner than saliva and too much of it.

Frank You're saying I'm no good.

Pitt I understand why they did it. Human beings lash out when they feel powerless and full of hate. We did that. Who are we? What do we know about civilisation? We're in the process of dismantling it.

Gray That is a point of view. Frank, I don't think you were ever going to be suitable. I'm sorry.

Frank I am. I am suitable.

Pitt Dream on, Frank.

Frank I'm not leaving. I want to see someone.

Pitt The bird. Show it to me, Frank.

Frank I don't know what you're talking about.

Pitt Dr Gray saw it too.

Gray The one you stole, Frank.

Pitt The artefact.

Gray It's in your pocket.

Pitt Frank, the bird.

Frank You are demonstrating an extreme bias, Doctor, you've taken against me. Why? You have a hidden agenda. It's your job against mine.

Pitt Show it to the camera, Frank.

He takes out the bird. He places it on the table.

You saw something in it. You had, let us say, a passionate response.
  You don't really want to be here. And now, really, you can't be.

Frank Where am I going to go?

Pitt You could say I'm saving you, Frank.

He takes the table centrepiece and holds it over the bird.

Pitt What are you doing?

Frank Stay away. Don't you think I can do it?

Gray Oh, my God.

Frank I don't want to, but . . .

Gray Wow!

Pitt Don't even think about it, Frank.

Gray That is like fucking apocalyptic!

Frank I don't want to, but I don't see any alternative.

Pitt Frank. Look at me. Remember those breathing techniques.

Frank I think I can do it.

Gray It would be something to see.

Frank I want to make something of my life.

Pitt Frank. Have mercy. There are some things I can't face being responsible for.
  Please.

Gray Fucking go for it, Frank.

Pitt Don't kill me, Frank.

Frank Sorry.

Pitt No, no!

  Frank lifts the centrepiece and smashes the bird.
    Pause.

Gray Just incredible.

Pitt Jesus, Frank. What did you do?

Frank I'm proving to you that I can do it.

Pitt God, Frank. What did you do?

Gray It's OK. It's OK. No one outside this building will know.

Pitt What did you do, Frank? It's in pieces.

Frank I gave it a pretty big smash.

Dr Pitt begins to scrabble around for the pieces.

Gray Don't overreact, Jacqueline.

Pitt That is a world destroyed.

Gray It was a piece of rock. The camera is running.

Dr Pitt continues to scrabble around for the pieces.

Frank I completed the task.

Gray You did, Frank, you did.

Frank Do you think I'm the kind of person they want?

Gray Yes, I think you are.

They exit.
  *Dr Pitt stays on her own with the pieces of bird.
  She has a physical reaction, like a small fit. As she
  recovers she hears around her the beating of wings.
  She looks up.*